*Two Plays*

# NANA
# GERMINAL

# NANA

*Adapted by Olwen Wymark*

# GERMINAL

*Adapted by William Gaminara*

*Two stage adaptations from
the novels of Emile Zola*

# NANA

# INTRODUCTION

Zola collaborated on a stage version of NANA in 1881. It was a moderate success (Zola's anxious questions to the director on the opening night – 'Did we cover our costs?') but it had nothing like the popularity of the adaptations of L'ASSOMMOIR, GERMINAL and THÉRÈSE RAQUIN.

This is rather surprising as the novel itself had been an absolute sensation the year before, devoured by the public, savaged as obscene and degenerate by the critics and even banned in England, its publisher actually jailed.

Certainly the book isn't particularly strong on suspense or plot. It's the history of a high class prostitute who rises from the vicious poverty of the urban working class to become first a not very talented actress and then a highly successful courtesan, the rage of Paris, who eats up the fortunes of aristocrats, playboys and bankers. At the height of her powers she dies hideously of smallpox.

Nana was Zola's symbol for the greed, debauchery and sexual hysteria of Paris in the Second Empire. His own summing-up of the book: 'A whole society hurling itself at the cunt. A pack of hounds after a bitch who is not even in heat. The poem of male desires.'

There is little development of or psychological exploration into the central characters. On the card in his files describing his heroine Zola says 'She is nothing but flesh, but flesh in all its beauty. A bird brain, very merry, very gay, never does harm for harm's sake but ends up regarding man as material to exploit and becomes a force of Nature, a ferment of destruction. She eats up gold and swallows up wealth. She makes a rush for pleasures and possessions and leaves nothing but ashes. But, above all else, a good natured girl.'

As always, Zola amassed a vast amount of documentary material before undertaking the actual composition of the book. He haunted the variety theatres and the fashionable cafés frequented by the *jeunesse dorée*. He took detailed notes of the lives and deaths of the great *demi-mondaines*. He persuaded a famous cocotte to show him over her entire mansion including her bedroom where he wrote a meticulous description of her splendidly ornate bed which he gave to Nana in his novel. He also read exhaustively in medical journals about the physical effects of smallpox, even visiting the morgue to view bodies of its victims; the last page of the book is a horrific description of Nana's corpse deformed and rotted by the disease.

The defeat of Napoleon III in the bloody welter of the Franco-Prussian War and the collapse of the Second Empire provides, with Nana's own collapse and death, a finale to the story. Zola points to the moral corruption and frantic greed for luxury exemplified in Nana's life as the cause of the destruction of this society.

There seem to be some echoes of our own compulsively consumerist society, our devoted pursuit of pleasures and possessions, and it was partly this that attracted Directors Sue Lefton and Jane Gibson to the idea of a new dramatisation of NANA. Choreographers as well as directors, they could also see the visual potential and ways of marrying music, dance and movement with the story. They asked me to write an adaptation of the novel for a production by the Shared Experience Theatre Company. Anthony Ingle was commissioned to compose the music which would weave in and out of the action as well as the score and lyrics of the pastiche operetta at the opening of the play.

My main difficulty was finding ways to strip down the rich and burgeoning life of the book into a fluent and fast moving dramatic text. It was necessary to keep the dialogue as spare as possible while not losing the texture and tone of the original. One great problem was how to translate the street language, the racy slang of the theatre world and the intimate jargon of the courtesans into language that didn't come over as archaic and quaint on the one hand or too jarringly modern on the other.

Equally one didn't want to venture into a kind of pretend French decorated with Gallic mannerisms and phrases. I read every translation of the novel I could find, experimented with vocabulary and pace and was still rewriting some of the speeches during the rehearsal period.

In this kind of adaptation it seems to me pointless to attempt to recreate a literary masterpiece. As Zola himself found in his dramatisations of his novels, almost all of his mesmerising descriptive language, much of the introspective life of his characters and, in fact, a great many of the characters themselves (our original cast list totalled well over forty) have to be sacrificed. The task is to exploit action and feelings and combine them with a sense of immediacy.

What I was not trying to do was to dramatise the novel as one would for television or radio but to put together a speakable and dramatic text which could be used to convert NANA into a piece of theatre.

OLWEN WYMARK

NANA was given its British première in this translation by the Shared
Experience Theatre Company in October 1987 at Winchester Theatre
Royal. It then moved to London to the Almeida Theatre in November
1987 and was subsequently transferred to the Mermaid Theatre in
February 1988 by Frank and Woji Gero. The cast included:

| | |
|---|---|
| FANTON, DAGEUNET, MARS | John Baxter |
| FAUCHERY, CHOUARD, PHILIPPE, NEPTUNE | Christian Burgess |
| NANA, VENUS | Belinda Davison |
| ROSE, SABINE, LA TRICON, DIANA | Lorna Heilbron |
| JUPITER, BORDENAVE, STEINER, GERARD | John Joyce |
| BLANCHE, SATIN, FERNANDE, CHEZELLES, MINERVA | Emma Longfellow |
| MUFFAT, LABORDETTE, OLD BOSC, VULCAN | Peter Sproule |
| TATAN NÉNÉ, MADAME LERAT, ESTELLE, MATHILDE, CERES | Julia St John |
| ZOE, MADAME HUGON, LUCY, SIMONNE, JUNO | Sandra Voe |
| GEORGES, VENOT, PRINCE, CUPID | Matthew Wadsworth |
| | |
| DIRECTED BY | Jane Gibson and Sue Lefton |
| COMPOSER AND MUSICAL DIRECTOR | Anthony Ingle |
| DESIGNER | Kenny Miller |
| LIGHTING DESIGNER | Ben Ormerod |

# ACT ONE

*Onstage are three large pillars, one upstage centre and the others further downstage on each side. At the back upstage on either side are two dressing room areas which are partly visible to the audience and partly concealed by screens and the side pillars. The actors use these spaces to change costume, wait for entrances etc. The screens are utilized in the action at points during the play to designate locations and define areas. There is another screen which is mirrored on one side and used in some scenes.*

*The stage is bare except for a central diagonal line of ten gold chairs. We are in the Théâtre des Variétés in Paris 1868. Fauchery enters from upstage, strolls round, regards the audience and goes to sit in one of the chairs. During the scene the four other men and the five women enter and move around the stage as required by the text.*

GEORGES: *(Excitedly to Fauchery.)* Have you met her? Do you know her? What's she like? The new star, I mean. Nana!

FAUCHERY: *(Bored)* My God, everybody in Paris today . . . Nana this, Nana that. Don't ask me. Nana's something Bordenave's invented. Ask him. It's his theatre.

BORDENAVE: Hey, Fauchery! What about that article you promised me? I open Figaro this morning – nothing!

FAUCHERY: Tomorrow. After I've seen your Nana. Meet Georges Hugon. It's his very first first night.

GEORGES: I'm awfully glad to meet you, Monsieur Bordenave. I think your theatre is absolutely marvellous!

BORDENAVE: You mean my brothel! *(Goes to side.)* What? No. Completely sold out!

FAUCHERY: Now then, Daguenet, what's this chat about you and the amazing Nana?

DAGUENET: All true.

BORDENAVE: No, not a seat in the house. Well, you should have booked ahead like everybody else.

FAUCHERY: And?

DAGUENET: *(Laughs. Kisses his fingers.)* Amazing!

> *At some point in this scene we hear sounds of the*
> *orchestra tuning up. This continues throughout until*
> *the overture.*

LUCY:       Nana? That Russian who set her up in her flat has
            deserted her, you know.

BLANCHE:    Well, it was the streets before he came along. She used
            to hang around outside the Papillon Club. She's not
            very bright. Pretty enough, I suppose.

LUCY:       Well . . . eighteen years old. *(To Faucher.)* Where are
            we sitting, sweetheart?

FAUCHERY:   First tier. Evening, Blanche. What have you done with
            your Rumanian prince?

BLANCHE:    I made him stay in the box while I had a stroll round.
            He's the most boring man in the world.

LUCY:       Does he have as much money as they say he does?

BLANCHE:    More.

FAUCHERY:   He's waving at you, Blanche.

BLANCHE:    *(Blowing a kiss out front.)* Buffoon!

SABINE:     Father not here yet?

MUFFAT:     Joining us shortly. Always late. Why he wanted us to
            come.

SABINE:     Papa enjoys the theatre. He always says we have a duty
            to culture and the arts.

MUFFAT:     *(Scathing)* Culture!

TATAN:      *(Going to Daguenet.)* Hello, Mimi. Is she nervous?

DAGUENET:   Nana? You're joking. She hasn't got nerves.

LUCY:       Why didn't you tell me you knew Nana?

FAUCHERY:   Nana? Never set eyes on her.

LUCY:       Blanche told me you'd slept with her.

GEORGES:    *(To Bordenave.)* I can't wait to see Nana. Everyone
            says she's a simply wonderful singer.

BORDENAVE:  Tone deaf.

GEORGES:    But the most glorious actress in Paris!

BORDENAVE: No talent at all.

FAUCHERY: And you want a good notice from me?

BORDENAVE: Nana doesn't have to sing or act. She's got something else. Reeks of it!

DAGUENET: *(Bows)* Monsieur le Comte de Beuville. My dear Madame la Countess.

SABINE: Monsieur Daguenet, how nice to see you. It's been a long time.

LUCY: Tatan! Hello, darling.

BLANCHE: I thought you were in Bordeaux.

TATAN: He lost all his money at the Casino.

BORDENAVE: *(To Fauchery.)* You'll see. The moment Nana comes out on that stage they'll all have their tongues hanging out.

LUCY: *(Indicating Daguenet.)* Who's that?

TATAN: Nana's latest boyfriend. Very posh. *(Laughs)* And very poor.

BORDENAVE: That skin of hers . . . you want to take a bite out of it!

GEORGES: She'll really put your theatre on the map.

BORDENAVE: Call it my brothel!

> *Embarrassed again, Georges looks away. Sees Muffat. Bows.*

FAUCHERY: You know Count Muffat? Introduce me.

TATAN: Wait till you see my new boyfriend. He's one of the actors. He's so ugly!

LUCY: What a joke Rose Mignon playing Diana in this. The Goddess of Chastity!

BLANCHE: Did you know her rich banker friend's getting a roving eye? For Nana, wouldn't you know.

LUCY: Steiner? Rose's husband'll be livid if she loses him. He's the main family income.

TATAN: I think it's disgusting a man pimping for his own wife.

BLANCHE: Well . . . Mignon's a good businessman.

SABINE:        *(To Georges.)* I count on you and your mother for my next Tuesday. Perhaps Monsieur Fauchery?

FAUCHERY:      Enchanted.

TATAN:         *(To Daguenet.)* Mimi! Everybody's buzzing about Nana!

DAGUENET:      So they should. *(Tickles her.)* Buzz buzz buzz!

TATAN:         *(Laughs)* Stop it, Mimi!

DAGUENET:      *(Pointing out front.)* Who's that fellow in the second row with Caroline and her mother. Oh it's only Labordette.

TATAN:         Did you know that Caroline's mother's become her manager now?

FAUCHERY:      Makes sense. Keeps the business in the family.

LUCY:          So where did you discover this Nana of yours, Monsieur Bordenave?

BORDENAVE:     In the gutter.

BLANCHE:       *(To Lucy.)* Look. La Tricon.

LA TRICON:     *(To Tatan.)* I've got someone for you. Tomorrow afternoon.

TATAN:         *(Pouts)* I'm spending the day with my boyfriend.

LA TRICON:     *(Walks away.)* An American. In shipping. Half past three.

GEORGES:       *(To Muffat.)* It's thrilling isn't it. Nana's debut! She's the talk of Paris, you know. It's going to be terribly exciting!

MUFFAT:        *(Icy courtesy.)* Do you think so?

               *Music. At the sound of the overture all the actors go swiftly and excitedly to sit in the chairs. They are now not specific characters but members of the audience of the Théâtre des Variétés. They talk animatedly to each other, calling over their shoulders, laughing, shouting, sometimes standing up etc.*

1 :       It's all about the gods, this operetta.

2 :       What a crowd. The place is packed!

3 :       Who's ever heard of Nana?

4 :       Posters plastered all over town.

5 :       She comes from the slums, this Nana.

6 :       Who wrote the music?

7 :       Bordenave's spent a fortune.

8 :       Her father was a drunken builder.

9 :       Her mother was a cheap whore.

10 :      It's so hot!

11 :      All the critics in Paris are here.

12 :      Nana's going to be a hit!

13 :      She'll be a disaster. Never acted in her life.

14 :      She's playing Venus.

15 :      Nana! The Goddess of Love!

16 :      Blonde and buxom.

17 :      She's sensational!

18 :      A ball of fire!

19 :      Nana Nana!

20 :      *(All)* Let's see Venus! We want Nana! Nana! Nana!
         Nana!

> *There is a loud chord and they all get up immediately
> and flourishing the chairs in the air and shouting
> Nana's name they go off to the dressing room areas.
> Now they are the performers in the operetta. There is
> much movement and bustle between the two dressing
> rooms as they get into their costumes and bring on the
> set pieces for the operetta. These consist of a big cut
> out shell upstage centre (behind which is the actress
> playing Nana) and some cut out waves. During all this
> the actors speak the following:*

1 :          Where's my trident?

2 :          Powder my back will you, Mathilde?

3 :          Move Fanton, you're in my way.

4 :          About time I had my own bloody dressing room.

5 :          Give us a drop of your brandy, Bosc.

6 :          Could somebody else have a look in the mirror
             Simonne?

7 :          Have you looked out front? It's a huge house.

8 :          Remember Gerard, we're taking the last exit much
             slower.

9 :          They're playing it far too fast.

10 :         I need a pin. Have you got a pin, Rose?

11 :         No!

12 :         Here, I'll do it.

13 :         Have they called beginners yet?

14 :         Bags of time. Bags of time.

15 :         It has to be tighter.

16 :         If you have it that tight, you'll faint.

17 :         Will you tell them I need that in the wings for the
             quick change?

18 :         Full company on stage. On stage ladies and gentlemen,
             please.

19 :         God, I'm sweating like a pig in this costume.

20 :         Good luck, darling.

21 :         You too.

22 :         On stage, please!

*Music. The Blonde Venus.*

NEPTUNE :    You all know me; I'm Neptune,
             And I'm the god of the sea.
             The Greeks call me Poseidon,
             It's all the same to me.

It's all the same to me.
The gods are all my guests today,
And there's a party on the way.
We're glad you've come, we hope you'll stay
And join us in our feasting.

MARS:    I'm Mars, the god of war
And fighting wars is what I'm for.
That's exactly as it should be,
But it's wearing rather thin for me.
I'd be so happy never to hear another trumpet!
I'm fed up with arms unless they're full of crumpet.
I've got a date with Venus
Who's an astounding eyeful;
Her husband might object,
But to me that's the merest trifle.

VULCAN:    I'm Vulcan, the smith of the gods.
With most of the gods I'm at odds,
Because lots of them fancy my wife!
But I'll catch her at it yet,
In my magic golden net,
A lesson she'll remember all her life.
*(Pause)* But she's immortal . . . we're all immortal . . .
So much the better!

CUPID:    I'm Venus's little baby,
There's fun wherever I go.
I can change your life completely
With just one twang of my bow,
With just one twang of my bow!

JUPITER:    I'm Jupiter, I rule this lot
And you as well (though you may not
Be aware of that) and now I rule
We're going to have a party, a party, a party!

GODS:    We're going to have a party now everybody's here.
We've told our wives it's a conference,
A conference, a conference!
We're told our wives it's a conference
And so we're in the clear!

JUNO:    A conference, indeed! By Jove, we've a score to settle,
wouldn't you say, Diana?

DIANA:    To go hunting in the moonlight
          Is a mystic, magic pastime;
          But what happened to me last time
          Makes me swear I'll never go hunting again.
          I had cornered my quarry,
          A magnificent stag stood at bay;
          Then – Ah me!

GODDESSES: What?

DIANA:    Young Cupid appeared,
          And took a shot at me!
          Ah, the shame!
          Venus must bear the blame!
          My defeat's in the bag;
          I love a stag!

MINERVA:  This is past all endurance!
          I encourage all men to be wise,
          But the moment that Venus approaches
          Their brains give way to their eyes.

CERES:    It's all very well to be fertile,
          To sow in wisdom and reap in joy;
          But all too often the joy's in the sowing,
          And that in spite of everyone's knowing
          That the fruit will ripen in sorrow,
          Thanks to Venus and her boy!

JUNO:     This state of affairs must be brought to an end,
          Honour and constancy we shall defend!
          The gods' base desires will be frustrated,
          And love and truth emancipated!

GODDESSES: We know you're there!
          You can't call this a conference.
          Out with you now;
          We will not have this nonsense!
          Venus must be told;
          She'll bring the world to ruin;
          We all know what she's doing
          And it makes our blood run cold!

> *The shell opens to reveal Venus who steps out and
> dances during the following chorus.*

ALL:            When blonde Venus roams at evening
                To see and to be seen,
                Who can say where she may wander?
                Of love she is the queen.
                All unarmed, she bears a challenge
                To men whose blood is red,
                And each defeated warrior
                In her lap will lay his head.

VENUS:          *(Singing very out of tune.)*
                When blonde Venus prowls at midnight
                For her hero, 'tis the hour;
                Though his sword sleep in its scabbard
                She will draw forth all its power.
                The victor will be vanquished,
                But the loss will be his gain;
                Though he falls in the encounter
                He will rise to (fight again).

                *She fails to achieve the last high note so instead of the
                last two words she laughs delightedly. Then she dances
                again.*

GODS:           Venus, O Queen of the skies,
                For a glance from your eyes
                All men would gladly die
                To live and live again to die.

GODDESSES:      Ah Venus! Ah Venus, etc.

GODS:           Venus, your subjects adore you,
                And so we implore you,
                Do not leave us
                And bereave us of our joy;
                It would drive us insane
                In our constant refrain –

ALL:            Ah Venus, come, Venus come . . .

                *They go forward to surround her and hide her from
                view. Then they exit and in a very bright light Venus
                stands alone. She takes off her outer layer of veils and
                stands in one filmy garment smiling, with arms
                upraised. Music cuts out. Zoe comes on and puts a
                negligée on Nana. Three creditors come on, two
                carrying chairs, one a table.*

CREDITOR 1: She's not hiring one more of my carriages until my bills are paid!

CREDITOR 2: Seven hundredweight of coal!

CREDITOR 3: She owes me for three dresses and four bodices!

ZOE: Out! Out! Out! Madame can't see you now. Wait in the hall.

*She pushes them offstage. Nana moves across to her, yawning.*

NANA: What time is it, Zoe?

ZOE: Nearly noon, Madame.

NANA: He's gone then.

ZOE: Two hours ago. He said he knew you were tired so he wouldn't wake you.

NANA: I didn't even hear him get out of bed.

ZOE: He told me to say he'd come tomorrow.

NANA: Poor Mimi, I really should chuck him. He's completely broke again.

ZOE: Yes you should!

NANA: *(Defiant)* I love him! And he comes from one of the best families in France . . . oh! Tomorrow's Friday. The old publisher's coming. He's changed his day. We'll have a real mess if he runs into Mimi.

ZOE: *(Reproof)* Madame didn't tell me. So is the Dago still coming on Tuesdays?

NANA: No. He's coming tonight.

ZOE: Really Madame, how am I to arrange things if –

NANA: All right, all right. Who was that at the door?

ZOE: Creditors.

NANA: Ugh. Has the concierge been up about the rent?

ZOE: Not yet. She will be.

NANA: Oh God, if I could only get my hands on that bloody Russian!

ZOE:        *(Cheerful)* Don't worry, Madame. There'll be plenty of
            men to choose from after last night. What a triumph,
            eh?

NANA:       *(Sulky)* Maybe. But I need money now, don't I. All
            those men cheering and yelling and here I am without
            a penny. Have you got all the bills there? *(Takes them
            and leafs through impatiently.)* I've got to have some
            money today. I promised Auntie I'd give her the fare
            to go and fetch the baby.

ZOE:        Has Madame seen Figaro? *(Reads)* The new Venus . . .
            audience went wild . . . her succulent beauty . . .

NANA:       *(Grabs the paper.)* Let me see. Oh, good old Fauchery!
            "Nana a star"! I bet Rose Mignon had a sleepless
            night. *(Doorbell. Zoe goes to answer it.)* Tell them to go
            to hell! *(Laughs)* Nana!

ZOE:        *(Comes in, disapproving.)* It's a woman. *(Looks at card.)*
            A Madame Tricon.

NANA:       Oh, la Tricon . . . excellent! *(Bundling Zoe out.)* How
            stupid you are, Zoe. Always pretending you don't know
            who she is.

            *La Tricon comes in.*

NANA:       Madame.

LA TRICON:  Can you be free this afternoon?

NANA:       Yes. How much?

LA TRICON:  Four hundred francs. Two o'clock. Agreed?

NANA:       Agreed.

            *La Tricon writes something down.*

LERAT:      *(Offstage)* Nana? Nana, dear. *(Comes on.)*

NANA:       Oh good, Auntie, you got here. Madame Tricon, may I
            present my Aunt, Madame Lerat?

LERAT:      Honoured to make your acquaintance, Madame.

LA TRICON:  *(Inclines her head.)* I must go. I have several calls to
            make.

            *Goes.*

LERAT:      Such elegant friends you have, dear girl. Zoe tells me
            you had a great success last night. ( *Pause; trenchant.*)
            Men! Devils from the ankles up, all of them.

NANA:       That's not the hat I bought for you.

LERAT:      (*Triumph*) It is! I retrimmed it.

NANA:       (*Annoyed*) It didn't need retrimming. It was perfectly –

LERAT:      (*Complacent*) I like to look smart, dear. I must be off
            soon, you know. The train goes at half past one.

NANA:       You'll have to catch a later one. I won't have the
            money till this afternoon. That wet nurse wants three
            hundred francs, you know.

LERAT:      All they care about is money. He'll be far better off
            with me.

NANA:       (*Fond*) As soon as he catches sight of me. . . . 'Mama!
            Mama!'

LERAT:      Bless him. By the way, who was baby's father?

NANA:       What? Oh . . . a gentleman.

LERAT:      I knew it. Shall little Louis and I be living here with
            you?

NANA:       No. I've found some rooms I'm going to rent for you.
            And I'll be giving you a hundred francs a month.

LERAT:      (*Shrieks. Embraces her.*) A hundred francs! Oh bleed
            those men white, Nana! Suck them dry!

ZOE:        If Madame is going out . . .

NANA:       Bugger. All right. Oh Auntie, I want you to write a
            letter for me. To my boyfriend.

LERAT:      (*Sentimental*) Ahhhhh . . .

NANA:       (*As Zoe dresses her.*) Tell him not to come tomorrow
            because the bloody old publisher'll be here.

LERAT:      (*Writing*) Dearest man of my heart . . . impossible to
            meet tomorrow, beloved . . .

NANA:       Tell him I miss him.

LERAT:      But you are near me whether near or afar –

NANA:       And give him lots of kisses.

LERAT:      A thousand kisses on your beautiful eyes.

NANA:       Lovely, Auntie.

LERAT:      Shall you sign it, dear?

NANA:       No, you do it. Zoe, get it off this afternoon will you?
            I'd better go I suppose. *(Pouts)* I don't want to. *(Sits)*

LERAT:      Now now, dear. When duty calls . . .

NANA:       Oh all right. *(Gets up.)* Zoe, we might have some callers
            today, don't you think?

ZOE:        I'm sure of it, Madame.

NANA:       Well, make them wait. *(Starts out.)*

ZOE:        The back stairs, Madame. Those creditors are in the
            front hall.

NANA:       *(Going out.)* Fucking vultures. I hate them.

            *Zoe puts things away. Madame Lerat lays out solitaire
            cards.*

LERAT:      Where did you work before you came here if you don't
            object to my enquiring?

ZOE:        For Madame Blanche de Sivry. I was with her for two
            years. She's forever begging me to go back to her –
            *(Doorbell. Zoe goes. Ushers Georges across the stage. He
            holds a bouquet. She indicates a place for him to stand.
            Returning.)* But I tell her I'm well suited here. Oh
            there's plenty of ladies would like to give me a situation
            but my opinion is – *(Doorbell. She goes. Brings on
            another man. Indicates a place to him. Comes back.)* –
            that  this is the best position for me in Paris. I believe
            in Madame Nana's future and I know I can help her to
            be  – *(Doorbell. It's another man and she does as before.
            Returning.)* – sensible and businesslike. *(Doorbell again
            so she just keeps on walking. Comes back with bouquet.)*
            Only a bouquet.

LERAT:      Oh if I had one tenth of the money men in Paris spend
            on flowers . . . such a waste. Red jack on black queen.
            Sit down for a moment. You must be worn out.

| | |
|---|---|
| ZOE: | *(Starts to sit.)* Well only for a – |
| | *Doorbell again. She goes.* |
| LERAT: | *(Shakes her head, laughing.)* La la la . . . |
| ZOE: | *(Leads on another man and places him. Coming back.)* Would you believe, Madame! It's that banker, Monsieur Steiner. He's Madame Rose Mignon's gentleman. |
| LERAT: | No! |
| ZOE: | Very wealthy. |
| LERAT: | Well that's nice. Black queen on red king . . . |
| | *Doorbell again. Zoe brings in another bouquet.* |
| ZOE: | Only another bouquet. *(Doorbell)* Well if that's another caller he'll have to go in the spare bedroom. *(Brings on fifth man. Places him.)* I've got one in every room now and it's not good policy to put two in together. *(Sits)* |
| | *The five men stand in and around Nana's room silent and waiting. Lerat and Zoe behave as if they aren't there.* |
| LERAT: | I shall miss my train . . . |
| ZOE: | Usually when Madame has an afternoon appointment she's hardly any time at all. |
| LERAT: | I haven't got a single ace out, drat it. |
| ZOE: | But look . . . the ten, nine and eight there . . . the jack on the queen . . . move these on to here . . . |
| LERAT: | *(Doing this, laughs.)* Ah ha! |
| | *Nana comes in, breathless and untidy.* |
| ZOE: | Madame is very late. |
| LERAT: | Naughty girl. |
| NANA: | Oh, piss off! Do you think I was having fun? Slobbering old fool. I thought I'd never get away. And then I couldn't get a taxi. |
| ZOE: | There are gentlemen waiting to see you. |
| NANA: | Well they can just bloody well go on waiting. |

| | |
|---|---|
| Zoe: | *(Significant)* Monsieur Steiner is here. |
| Nana: | What? Rose Mignon's old banker? Oh won't she be mad. *(Bad-tempered again.)* I suppose he thinks he can do anything he wants just because of his measly bouquet last night. Well I don't want to see him. Boring old fart. |
| Zoe: | *(Firm)* Madame will reconsider and Madame will see Monsieur Steiner. |
| Nana: | Shan't! |
| Zoe: | *(Shrugs)* And the Dago has arrived early. |
| Nana: | Oh has he. Well he can go too! They can all go. I'm not seeing anyone. |

*Doorbell again. Zoe goes.*

| | |
|---|---|
| Lerat: | Did you get the money? |
| Nana: | What a question. *(Takes money from her bosom.)* Here you are. Three hundred for the nurse and fifty for your fare. I'm keeping fifty for myself. |
| Zoe: | *(Coming in.)* Two gentlemen. I've told them Madame will receive them in the drawing room shortly. |
| Nana: | *(Angrily)* Oh you did, did you. I suppose you're the mistress here and I'm the bloody maid. I said I – |
| Zoe: | *(Hands her two visiting cards.)* The Count Muffat de Beuville and the Marquis de Chouard. |
| Nana: | Oh. |
| Lerat: | Fancy. Noblemen! The Marquis de Chouard . . . |
| Zoe: | *(Demure)* They said they were collecting for charity. |
| Nana: | Charity my ass! |

*Now all four actresses come down to join her. They are now all Nana. They take lines of the speech alternately or in chorus. They are all physically linked . . . touching each other. After the last line of the speech Lerat and Zoe return to former positions and the other two actresses go off.*

ALL:          They're after what all the rest of them are after.
              Strutting in here with their cocks stuck out in front of
              them. Oh Nana, look what I've got for you! Drooling
              and shaking so much they can hardly get their clothes
              off. Oh it's so exciting for me to have them sweating
              and thrashing around all over me. Such a thrill to see
              their big white bottoms pumping up and down and
              listen to them grunting and groaning and snorting like
              dying pigs. And I have to lie there pretending to be
              wild with passion. Making silly little moans and gasps
              and writhing with joy. Great greedy guzzleguts. Snuffle
              snuffle snuffle! Gobble gobble gobble! Give me give
              me give me! Oh lucky Nana! Like shit.

ZOE:          *(Back in place.)* Madame!

NANA:         Don't Madame me. Anyway that's just the kind of talk
              they love.

LERAT:        But it's not nice, darling. It's common.

NANA:         Sorry I was cross, Zoe. Where are the bloody old
              lechers? In the front room?

ZOE:          The *drawing* room, Madame. No. Wait. I'll show them
              in here.

NANA:         Good idea.

ZOE:          *(Bundling Lerat off.)* Off you go. Into the kitchen.

              *She goes and ushers the two men to Nana. Then goes
              off pushing one of the others off before her.*

NANA:         Gentlemen. Forgive me for keeping you waiting.

MUFFAT:       *(Not quite looking at her.)* I hope you will pardon our
              intrusion, Madame, but my father-in-law and I are
              members of the Charities Committee for the district.

CHOUARD:      When we heard a famous artiste lived in this house we
              felt sure we would not ask in vain. Great talent means a
              great heart.

NANA:         *(Gracious)* Of course one is only too happy to give to
              the poor.

CHOUARD:      *(Coming closer.)* And such poverty, Madame. You can't
              imagine the misery. Children with nothing to eat,

mothers ill with consumption, babies dying of the
cold . . .

NANA:          *(Genuine distress.)* Oh the poor little souls! *(Then taking
money from her bosom seductively.)* I'm afraid this is all I
have in the house at present but you're welcome to it
for such a good cause.

               *Holds out the money to Muffat who takes it nervously.
               She smiles at him. He turns away confusedly.*

MUFFAT:        Madame is too generous. We must go.

               *He blunders out. Chouard follows but turns and winks
               and licks his lips salaciously at Nana.*

NANA:          *(When they've gone.)* Dirty old rat! *(Laughs)* Men taking
money from me! *(Thoughtful)* The Count Muffat de
Beuville . . . *(Zoe comes back in.)* So? Have you thrown
the rest of them out?

ZOE:           I put Monsieur Steiner into the drawing room in case
you'd changed your –

NANA:          Well I haven't. Get rid of him.

ZOE:           Has Madame really thought about all the –

NANA:          Go and tell him to get out.

ZOE:           But –

NANA:          If I want to get him, the best way is to kick him out
first.

ZOE:           Ah . . .

               *Zoe goes and ushers Steiner out. Nana gets up and
               dances round as if looking into rooms.*

NANA:          No one in the morning room . . . no one in the drawing
room . . . and now there's no one in the – *(Encountering
Georges.)* My God! There's still one here. *(He jumps,
startled. She laughs.)* Are they sending me children
now? Do you want me to blow your nose, baby?

GEORGES:       *(Faint with joy.)* Yes!

NANA:          Now then. What's your name and now old are you?

GEORGES:       *(Breathless)* Georges Hugon. Nearly seventeen.

NANA:        Are those flowers for me? *(He nods.)* Well give them to
             me. *(She tries to take them but he falls on his knees and
             seizes her hands, kissing them frantically.)* Stop, you little
             monster, stop it! *(Cuffs him.)* Really! A baby like you
             behaving like a – *(But she's pleased. Pats his cheek.)* Get
             up, silly. Now run along home to your Mama. *(Pushes
             him out.)* Don't fuss. You can come and see me again.
             Satisfied?

GEORGES:     Yes!

                 *He reels out. Zoe comes on.*

ZOE:         Another gentleman, Madame.

NANA:        Oh Zoe! *(Then delighted.)* Oh, it's only Labordette!

LABORDETTE: *(Cheerful)* Only me. Well dear girl, you seem to have
             become the most famous infamous woman in Paris.

NANA:        I don't know who you're calling infamous. I've had
             titled gentlemen here today. And Steiner came to call.

LABORDETTE: Oh well done. You couldn't do better. How's Daguenet
             going to take it?

NANA:        Mimi? He won't mind. *(Doorbell)* Zoe, don't let anyone
             else in! That bastard Bordenave giving my address to
             the whole world!

LABORDETTE: Well the concierge is very impressed. Not to mention
             the creditors.

NANA:        *(Laughs)* Oh good. Let's have supper together before
             the theatre, Labordette. I'm not on till after nine.

ZOE:         *(Comes in, harried.)* I said you weren't at home but
             more keep coming all the time! *(A line of the other four
             actors forms behind her.)* There's a queue of them
             halfway down the stairs. They won't leave.

NANA:        Well let them stay out there. *(Zoe goes out.)* Aren't you
             glad you're not part of that pack of idiots always
             sniffing around after us?

LABORDETTE: Less tiring just to be friends.

NANA:        *(Friendly)* Friends because we're your ticket to the best
             society in Paris.

LABORDETTE : Don't be cynical sweetheart. You know I adore you.

ZOE :        (*Comes in.*) Oh Madame, I forgot to mention. The Dago can't come round tonight.

NANA :       Oh hooray! When I get home tonight I can go to bed all by myself.

*She dances out after Zoe. Sabine, Muffat and their daughter Estelle come on. Music. During the slow introduction the rest of the company come on as guests to Sabine's party. Nana watches, separate from the scene. The men are Steiner, Fauchery, Daguenet and Venot. The women Baroness Chezelles and Madame Hugon. After silent and formal greetings they form couples and, with the exception of Venot, go into a quadrille. After the dance there is another silence during which Sabine goes and takes Madame Hugon by the hands.*

SABINE :     It's so lovely to see you, dear Madame Hugon. You hardly ever come up from the country these days.

HUGON :      I simply had to make a trip to the world exhibition.

SABINE :     They say the Shah of Persia will be here, you know.

CHEZELLES : I believe the King of Prussia is coming too.

*The dialogue in this scene is slow and formal with pauses. At certain points Daguenet, Fauchery and Steiner speak confidentially to each other. They should do this without resorting to stage whispers or asides. It's clear that the other characters don't hear these speeches.*

FAUCHERY :   There's a rumour that the exhibition may not be ready on time.

MUFFAT :     (*Severe*) It will be ready. That is the Emperor's wish.

SABINE :     Count Bismarck is going to accompany the King of Prussia, I understand.

STEINER :    Charming man.

DAGUENET :   You know him, Steiner?

STEINER :    Very well. I often have business in Berlin.

CHEZELLES: I'm surprised you say charming, Monsieur. I lunched with Bismarck at my brother's house last year. I found him boorish.

DAGUENET: You're too hard on him, Baroness. Count Bismarck can be a very witty man.

STEINER: And he's a very wealthy one.

CHEZELLES: People are saying that he means to make war on us.

HUGON: *(Horrified)* Oh surely not. Not a war!

SABINE: Do you think that could be possible, my dear?

MUFFAT: Certainly not. Fortunately we have the Emperor to protect us.

SABINE: Yes we do. God be thanked.

HUGON: *(Relieved)* Yes.

DAGUENET: Your son Georges didn't come with you this evening, Madame Hugon?

HUGON: Not well, Monsieur Daguenet. A little feverish. He overtires himself studying. He was looking forward to seeing little Estelle again. *(Pats her hand.)* Such a grown up young woman now.

SABINE: Estelle dear, show Madame Hugon your tapestry.

STEINER: Have you heard about the latest fluctuations on the stock market, Count?

MUFFAT: *(Repressive)* No.

STEINER: I understand it might be very shrewd to invest in steel

MUFFAT: *(Moves away.)* I'm afraid I have no idea.

VENOT: Worldly matters, Monsieur Steiner. Investments . . . money . . .

STEINER: Well take my word for it, the world would be in a pretty fix without the stock market.

SABINE: Monsieur Fauchery, I think you've not met our old friend, Monsieur Venot.

FAUCHERY: Of course I've heard of you Monsieur . . . though, forgive me, I had thought you were a man of the cloth.

VENOT:        No no, a retired lawyer. Now a mere churchwarden.

SABINE:       Mere!

MUFFAT:       Monsieur Venot is the most profoundly moral man of
              my acquaintance. A true Christian and a great example
              in these loose times.

VENOT:        You overestimate me, my dear friend.

MUFFAT:       Indeed I do not. You have always been my most valued
              spiritual guide.

CHEZELLES:    I thought we were to see the Marquis de Chouard
              tonight, Sabine.

SABINE:       He promised faithfully he'd come. Poor father, I'm
              afraid he's had to work late at the ministry.

VENOT:        A most dedicated man.

DAGUENET:     *(To Fauchery. Unheard by the others.)* Oh very
              dedicated. I've heard 'poor father' works late with a
              fifteen year-old tart these days.

FAUCHERY:     That's right. Likes them young and mucky does the
              Marquis de Chouard. Has the Countess Sabine got a
              lover?

DAGUENET:     Good God no, are you mad? She's as pious and
              strait-laced as her husband.

FAUCHERY:     There's something about her.

DAGUENET:     But has she got thighs?

FAUCHERY:     I'll let you know.

DAGUENET:     You won't. The woman's made of ice.

FAUCHERY:     *(Glance at the count.)* Well . . . married to that.

DAGUENET:     Yes. She was only seventeen when they married her off
              to him. Actually, I heard . . . *(Can't go on for laughing.)*

FAUCHERY:     You heard what?

DAGUENET:     That he was a virgin when he married her.

FAUCHERY:     *(Laughs)* Impossible!

DAGUENET:     I assure you. Hadn't the first idea how to do it!

MUFFAT: Is your elder son Philippe in Paris, Madame Hugon?

HUGON: No, he's still garrisoned at Bourges. He's doing so well in the army. They think very highly of him.

SABINE: And young Georges going into the law?

HUGON: Yes, but he still seems a baby to me. He insisted on taking me to the theatre the other night. Something about Gods and Goddesses. I can't say I enjoyed it but he was so happy. The child simply adores music.

*Fauchery and Daguenet smile at each other.*

DAGUENET: *(Excitedly. Unheard by the others.)* Tomorrow night! Nana's party! Are you going?

MUFFAT: You must be proud of your sons, Madame.

FAUCHERY: *(To Daguenet.)* Do you think I'd miss it?

HUGON: Yes, I'm a very fortunate mother.

STEINER: Midnight! After the theatre! At her house!

CHEZELLES: Did you hear? Baroness Fougeray's daughter has taken the veil. Such a sad business.

DAGUENET: *(To Steiner.)* You're going, Steiner? What about your dear Rose Mignon?

VENOT: Sad, Madame? The church teaches us it's an occasion for rejoicing.

STEINER: *(To Daguenet.)* Oh Rose is going with her husband.

SABINE: But so young. Only seventeen. *(Pause)* Estelle, dear, won't you sing us something?

*Music.*

ESTELLE: Now as the sun sinks in the west,
Crimson in his evening glory,
His radiance falls on the lake,
Kindling its depths to fire.
Just so is our love,
As it draws us together,
Set ablaze by the glory of heaven
In the soul's purest desire.

*Polite applause.*

FAUCHERY:       *(Applauding. To Daguenet.)* Christ! What a dreary piece! *(Laughs)* No singing virgins tomorrow night!

STEINER:        *(Glee)* Nana invited me to the party herself!

VENOT:          We should envy Mademoiselle Fougeray her vocation.

SABINE:         Oh yes . . . yes.

FAUCHERY:       *(To Daguenet.)* How many will be there?

DAGUENET:       Twenty or so, I should think.

MUFFAT:         Indeed. A life of prayer and meditation. Beautiful.

FAUCHERY:       Same old set of women I suppose.

STEINER:        Actresses! Courtesans!

HUGON:          I'm afraid it seems cruel to me. A child doing that to her parents . . . an enclosed order. It's like suicide.

MUFFAT:         God in his wisdom has chosen her, Madame.

VENOT:          Amen.

HUGON:          Yes, of course.

FAUCHERY:       *(To Daguenet.)* You'll never guess who Nana asked me to invite.

                *He moves to stand by Muffat who is unaware of him.*

DAGUENET:       I don't believe you! She didn't tell me.

STEINER:        He'd never accept!

                *The three men stand round the Count.*

FAUCHERY:       Let's try him. Monsieur le Comte . . . *(Muffat turns to look at him.)* There's a lady who would like to have you for supper tomorrow night, Count.

MUFFAT:         What do you mean? Who?

DAGUENET:       Why, Nana. From the Théâtre des Variétés.

MUFFAT:         *(Brief pause.)* I am not acquainted with that . . . lady.

DAGUENET:       *(Innocent)* But surely you've called at her house.

MUFFAT:         What? Oh . . . the other day . . . I'd forgotten. That was on behalf on the Charities Committee.

FAUCHERY:       May I tell her you'll come?

MUFFAT:     No! *(Embarrassed by his vehemence.)* No.

DAGUENET:   But it's to be a party for artists, Count. Surely talent
            cuts across all the class barriers nowadays. Some titled
            people will be there. And the Spanish ambassador, I
            believe.

MUFFAT:     *(Wavering)* I see. Well, perhaps I – *(Venot has got up.
            Stands behind Muffat. Now puts his hand on his shoulder.
            The music which has been playing under the scene stops. A
            silence.)* No! Impossible!

> *Music. The next scene, Nana's party, is improvised by
> the actors and musicians. It is in every way the
> opposite of Sabine's staid polite salon. It is anarchic,
> orgiastic and ludicrous. The actors all become party-
> goers, waiters, courtesans etc. and as the music starts
> Nana comes running in amongst them. The actors
> respond to the music and the music to the actors. There
> is a surrealist "Dada-ist" tone. Elements of the
> activity include meeting and greeting, eating and
> drinking, lewd sexual play and voyeurism. Noise and
> chatter. A few phrases stand out. Early in the scene
> Nana shouts out 'Everyone sit where they like'. Lines
> which can be used in the first section:*

1:          No place cards. How quaint.

2:          Carp à la Chambord?

3:          Second-rate champagne of course.

4:          Really! She's got the manners of a skivvy!

> *This last when Nana, losing her temper as the party
> gets rowdier, stamps out.*

NANA:       This is what I get for inviting this filthy mob to my
            house!

> *She stands angrily downstage tossing her head,
> stamping her foot. Daguenet runs over to her to
> expostulate and try to get her to come back but she
> resists him. Steiner reels over to her shouting.*

STEINER:    Nana! Nana! Nana!

> *The party carries noisily on but Nana turns and seizes
> Steiner.*

NANA:        Steiner! Will you buy me a country house?

STEINER:     The biggest one I can find.

NANA:        I want gardens and fountains and fields for acres and acres as far as you can see.

STEINER:     Acres and acres and acres . . .

NANA:        And a flock of sheep and my very own herd of cows.

STEINER:     *(Groping her breasts and buttocks.)* Yes yes yes! Cows and sheep and swans and goldfish and – *(A cry.)* A pin! I've pricked myself!

NANA:        Now the bargain's sealed in blood!

             *Steiner embraces her drunkenly his head on her breast.*

DAGUENET:    *(Maudlin)* Oh Nana, I've lost you. What shall I do without you?

NANA:        Don't be silly, Mimi. Nothing's changed between you and me. Kiss me. *(He does.)* Oh harder than that! Harder, Mimi, harder!

STEINER:     *(Groaning with desire.)* Oh harder, yes! Yes, harder! Let's go to bed, Nana!

NANA:        I don't want to go to bed. Take me to the Bois de Boulogne and we can watch them do the milking.

STEINER:     *(As she drags him off.)* But Nana –

NANA:        I want them to milk the cows in front of me!

             *They go off. By now everyone at the party is lying about drunk and exhausted. There is giggling and groaning and yawning. Again we hear a few phrases.*

1:           Give the piano some champagne.

2:           What a madhouse.

3:           Where's she gone?

4:           I feel sick.

5:           Champagne for the piano?

             *As the talk fizzles out to silence, the music fades down. Then a loud crashing chord. Everyone gets up at once and goes off. Now the sound of the orchestra tuning*

*up. We are again backstage at the theatre and the
evening performance is setting up.*

1 :        Bring the backdrop in.

2 :        Steady on those ropes.

3 :        Get the shell further upstage.

4 :        Bring in the batten. Lower! That's it.

5 :        Waves onstage, please. Go on, go on, get moving!

6 :        Can we have more light over here?

7 :        Clear the downstage entrances.

8 :        Clear the stage.

> *The above is to cover light change and the shifting of
> screens downstage, the mirrored one to form Nana's
> dressing room and another to suggest a dressing room
> for Fanton. Chouard comes through between them and
> is met by a stage hand.*

STAGE HAND: Who shall I say to Monsieur Bordenave?

CHOUARD :    The Marquis de Chouard. *(The stage hand goes.)*
             Muffat? Where have you got to?

MUFFAT :     I'd really rather not come with you. No, I won't come.

CHOUARD :    Of course you will. I told that fellow Bordenave we'd
             escort the Prince.

MUFFAT :     It's not suitable for us to be here. There might be talk.

CHOUARD :    Suitable for royalty but not for you, eh?

ROSE :       *(Walking across with Mathilde.)* If that Fanton's drunk
             in my scene again I'm going to Bordenave.

MATHILDE :   There's no bloody fire in the Green Room again.

MUFFAT :     Sabine will be expecting me.

> *Music. The overture.*

CHOUARD :    *(Ogling the actresses.)* All right!

SATIN :      *(Coming on. To actresses.)* Where's Nana's dressing
             room?

ROSE :       Over there.

*She and Mathilde go off.*

CHOUARD:     *(Drawn by Satin.)* There's a juicy little piece.

MUFFAT:      Sorry? What did you say?

CHOUARD:     Nothing. Nothing.

> *Bordenave comes on leading the prince obsequiously.*

BORDENAVE:   Please come this way, your Highness. If his Royal
             Highness would just step this way . . .

PRINCE:      Thank you.

STAGE HAND:  *(Offstage)* Get that shell out of the way.

BORDENAVE:   Take care, your Highness!

> *He takes the prince to Chouard and Muffat. They greet
> each other. Fanton comes running across to the side
> dressing room.*

BORDENAVE:   Overture's started, Fanton.

FANTON:      I know. I'm coming. *(Shouts into wings.)* Go to the café
             and get me a bottle of champagne, will you? It's my
             name day.

MATHILDE:    Wardrobe's waiting for you, Fanton.

FANTON:      All right, all right. Keep your hair on.

> *Overture fades out. Satin comes back on and goes into
> Nana's dressing room where Nana had been sitting
> making up her face.*

NANA:        Satin! Good girl. You came.

SATIN:       *(Laughs)* Hello you old cow!

> *They kiss.*

NANA:        I'm going to speak to Bordenave about fixing you up
             with something.

SATIN:       I'm not sure I want a bloody job. What would I do
             pissing around in a chorus? Anyway you know I've
             been tone deaf all my life.

NANA:        What does that matter? You'll make a lot of contacts
             here, Satin. It's better than the streets believe me.

BORDENAVE: *(Knocks on the door.)* Nana! His Royal Highness is here. He wants to visit you.

NANA: I'm not dressed!

SATIN: I'm off.

NANA: No, stay. Behind there. *(They both go behind the screen as Bordenave comes in with the prince, Chouard and Muffat. Fanton has left his dressing room. Nana, cross.)* Oh it's silly coming in like that.

BORDENAVE: Nana . . . it's his Highness! Come now, don't be childish. Out you come.

NANA: I won't!

BORDENAVE: Good heavens, these gentlemen know perfectly well what a woman looks like. They won't eat you.

PRINCE: I'm not so sure of that.

*Everyone laughs except Muffat.*

CHOUARD: An exquisite *mot*, Highness. Thoroughly Parisian.

*Nana comes out. She bobs a curtsey.*

NANA: Forgive me for receiving you like this, your Royal Highness . . .

PRINCE: It is I who have been importunate, Madame.

CHOUARD: *(Plucking at Bordenave.)* Thank you so much.

BORDENAVE: Oh. *(Disappointed)* If his Highness will excuse me . . . *(Sidles out.)*

NANA: *(As Chouard kisses her hand hungrily.)* Monsieur le Marquis. *(Sees Muffat.)* Count Muffat! I didn't see you there. I should scold you for not coming to my supper party.

CHOUARD: What? Refuse an invitation from Nana?

PRINCE: Fortunate to receive one.

MUFFAT: I . . . I . . . it's so hot in here!

*Music.*

FANTON: *(Coming to dressing room.)* Champagne! Champagne! I bring champagne! *(Bursts in. Stops short.)* Oh.

|          | *(Recovers. Very stagey.)* The God Mars wishes to toast his Royal Highness, the Prince from England! |
|----------|---|
| PRINCE:  | *(Laughing)* The Prince thanks the God Mars heartily. |
| NANA:    | *(Rubbing up against Fanton.)* It's Monsieur Fanton's name day. |
| FANTON:  | It is it is it is, my fair Venus. *(He kisses her on the lips. Muffat watches in a kind of torment.)* To Venus! |
| CHOUARD: | To Venus! |
| PRINCE:  | To Venus! |
| MUFFAT:  | *(With difficulty.)* To Venus. |
| CHOUARD: | *(Cackles)* Well done! Well done! |
| VOICE:   | *(Offstage)* Fanton! You're on . . . you're on. |
| FANTON:  | That's me. *(Goes out grinning.)* Salutations, Highness! |
| PRINCE:  | Many thanks, Mars! |

*All the men leave the dressing room opening the screen out to its full extent as they go. The other three women join Nana and Satin and all the women, in a bright light, face the mirror and slowly and voluptuously put on lipstick and fix their hair, bending and swaying. Muffat stands downstage in another light gazing at them. As the music reaches its pitch, the mirrored screen is lowered from behind and the five women turn to gaze sensuously and unsmiling at Muffat. He moves slowly towards Nana. The other men come on and each moves toward one of the women. Like Muffat they go down on their knees and crawl after the women. Then they are all still. The men gazing longingly up at the women, the women quite uninvolved. Muffat rises and stands looking helplessly at Nana. The music stops.*

| NANA: | I have a house in Orleans. It's quite near your friend, Madame Hugon's country place. Perhaps you'd like to visit me there. |
|---|---|
| ALL THE MEN: | Yes . . . |

*The women leave the men and go off. The men are left in attitudes of beseeching desire. A chord. The men get up at once and move swiftly offstage. The stage is empty. Sound of birdsong.*

NANA: *(Offstage. Shouts)* There's the house! Look, Zoe! There it is. *(Comes on. Zoe follows, bad-tempered.)* Oh isn't it big! And so chic. Look at that beautiful flowering vine!

ZOE: Bindweed, Madame.

NANA: It's a real mansion! *(Awe)* Honestly Zoe, doesn't it look exactly like a picture postcard?

ZOE: Yes, Madame.

NANA: Oh I love the country, don't you?

ZOE: I was born in it, Madame.

*Goes off.*

NANA: Lucky lucky you! The air smells so sweet. The trees and the grass . . . funny little hedges. Listen to those birds. Are they nightingales, Zoe?

ZOE: *(Off)* No, Madame.

NANA: I must see all over the house. Immediately!

ZOE: *(Off)* It's going to rain.

*Madame Hugon, Muffat and Sabine come onstage. Muffat is nervous and abstracted.*

SABINE: How lovely to be here again. Dear Madame Hugon. All those summers in my childhood.

HUGON: But we're having so much rain this Autumn. If only you could have come in June as you'd planned.

SABINE: We were all packed and ready but then the Count had urgent business. I was so happy when he discovered we could come this week.

HUGON: It was just the same with my Georges. He's been promising all summer to come down. *(As Georges comes on with Estelle.)* There you are, darling. Did you show Estelle the goldfish?

GEORGES: Yes, Maman.

HUGON: I was just saying I'd quite given up hope of seeing you. Then all of a sudden . . . here you are.

GEORGES:       I did write, Maman.

HUGON:         *(Laughs)* And the letter arrived five minutes before you
               did! He's a dear good sweet boy to bury himself in the
               country for his old mother's sake. *(Kisses him.)* My
               little Zizi. And I didn't tell you, Sabine, when your
               friend Monsieur Venot heard you were visiting me, he
               wrote to say he'd join us. Isn't that good news!

SABINE:        My dear, did you hear that? Monsieur Venot is coming
               down.

MUFFAT:        What's that? Venot? Oh good . . . good.

GEORGES:       *(As Daguenet comes on.)* I invited Monsieur Daguenet. I
               knew you wouldn't mind.

HUGON:         Of course not. Most welcome. *(As Fauchery comes on.)*
               And Monsieur Fauchery as well! I thought you weren't
               able to get away from Paris.

FAUCHERY:      Couldn't resist the temptation of the country, Madame.

HUGON:         I'm delighted. I'm usually starved for company down
               here and now suddenly a houseful! But we've had some
               bad news, I'm afraid. That banker person, Monsieur
               Steiner, has bought a country house not a mile from
               here. For an actress!

MUFFAT:        *(Mutters. Not meeting her gaze.)* Is that so?

FAUCHERY:      Really?

DAGUENET:      An actress?

HUGON:         That woman Georges and I saw at the theatre. What
               was her name, Georges?

GEORGES:       *(As if searching his mind.)* I can't just . . .

SABINE:        We saw  her too, didn't we my dear?

MUFFAT:        Did we? I can't remember . . .

HUGON:         Nana! That was it. Horrible creature.

GEORGES:       I've got rather a headache, Maman. I think it's a
               migraine coming on.

HUGON:         Oh Zizi, dear.

GEORGES:       I won't have any supper. I'll just go to bed.

HUGON:    I'll have a tray sent up.

GEORGES:  No no, don't bother. Food would make me sick. *(As he goes.)* I'll be quite all right if I can just get to sleep.

HUGON:    Poor darling. He's been overworking himself.

SABINE:   What a shame. Is this actress person in residence, Madame?

HUGON:    Well as a matter of fact I thought I saw her this afternoon but Georges assured me it wasn't her.

FAUCHERY: I shouldn't think a woman like that would want to leave Paris.

DAGUENET: That type usually loathes the country, you know.

*Georges circles round them as running to Nana's house.*

SABINE:   Well let's hope she doesn't come down while we're here.

HUGON:    Yes indeed!

NANA:     *(Running on. They don't notice her.)* Look! There's a great big huge kitchen garden. I'm going to look at it.

*Crosses and runs off.*

HUGON:    Well I've really no right to be angry. I should try to be more tolerant. We must live and let live, mustn't we, Monsieur.

MUFFAT:   Yes . . . yes of course.

NANA:     *(Coming into their midst.)* Strawberries in my own garden!

*Gets down to pick them.*

DAGUENET: *(Aside to Fauchery.)* She's coming down at the weekend.

FAUCHERY: With Steiner?

DAGUENET: Yes but he's no problem. Nana sees to that.

NANA:     Oh, they're so juicy!

*Hugon goes off with Sabine and Muffat and Estelle.*

FAUCHERY: I'm still quite fascinated by the Madame la Countess Sabine.

DAGUENET:   A contrast to her daughter. What a stick, eh?

FAUCHERY:   A stick with a dowry of eight hundred thousand.

DAGUENET:   *(Brief pause.)* Is that so?

          *They go.*

ZOE:        *(Offstage)* Come in, Madame. You'll be drenched and it's getting dark.

NANA:       *(Shouts)* Oh don't be such a spoilsport, Zoe!

GEORGES:    *(Running on.)* Nana!

NANA:       Georges!

GEORGES:    I've got away.

NANA:       Oh look at you, Zizi. You're soaking. You'll catch your death. Come inside quickly and we'll dry you in front of the fire.

          *They run off.*

          *Sabine comes on upstage. She stands slowly stroking her hair.*

MUFFAT:     *(Coming on downstage.)* I've come to say good night. *(She doesn't look at him or respond but strokes her hair, caresses her shoulders. After a pause.)* Well goodnight my dear. I hope you sleep well.

          *Again she is silent, absorbed. After another pause he goes.*

SABINE:     *(Not looking after him. Dreamy.)* Goodnight.

          *She goes slowly off as Nana and Georges come running on, laughing. He is wearing one of her petticoats and is twirling about.*

NANA:       Oh don't you make a lovely girl. Sweet thing. I'm going to call you Dolly. You're my own dear little girlfriend, aren't you Dolly?

GEORGES:    Little? I'm bigger than you.

NANA:       *(Pats her chest.)* Not here you aren't, Dolly.

GEORGES:    Yes, I am rather wanting there.

*She sits on the floor and holds her arms out to him.*
*The actress who plays Madame Hugon comes on*
*dressed the same as Nana and stands near them unseen*
*by them. Nana wants to play but Georges begins to get*
*excited and kisses and caresses her. She tries to push*
*him away.*

NANA: Stop it, you naughty boy. *(He goes on nuzzling her.)*
Stop it this minute.

*Nana pushes him toward Nana/Hugon who he*
*embraces on his knees in front of her.*

NANA/
HUGON: Leave me alone. You're too young. You must think of
me as your Mama.

GEORGES: Take me to bed, Nana.

NANA/
HUGON: No no. You're only a baby. A boy.

GEORGES: And you're the most beautiful girl in the world. So
sweet. So young.

NANA/
HUGON: Oh I am young, Zizi. I'm only a girl.

GEORGES: My girl. My sweetheart. I want you!

NANA/
HUGON: Oh my darling, we mustn't. It's wrong. It's wrong.

GEORGES: It's right! It's right! I love you. I'll always love you,
Nana.

*As he says this he turns from Nana/Hugon to Nana.*
*The former goes off. Georges and Nana lie on the floor*
*in a loving embrace. Muffat comes on on the other side*
*of the stage.*

MUFFAT: I haven't slept. I can't sleep. Whenever I close my eyes
I see her. . . . Nana! What on earth am I doing here? I
should never have come. Never. I must go. Leave.
Run. Run! Oh I want to hold her. . . . I want to touch
her . . . kiss her – My God, my God, out of the depths
I cry to thee. Help me, Lord! Oh her hair . . . those
shoulders . . . her naked belly – the Whore of Babylon!
Save me, Father, save me! *(Groans)* I want to tear her

clothes, I want to bite her breasts . . . drown myself
inside her! *(Cries out.)* Christ have mercy on me!
*(Resolve)* Church. . . . I'll go to Mass. Yes. I must go to
Mass.

*Music. Muffat crosses himself and kneels upstage.
Sabine, Fauchery, Estelle, Daguenet and Madame
Hugon come on.*

SABINE:      Oh smell the air, Estelle! What a wonderful morning!

FAUCHERY:    *(Looks at her, his face close to hers.)* Beautiful.

*Estelle stares at him suspiciously.*

HUGON:       Thank heaven the rain's stopped. *(As George comes on,
yawning.)* How is your head dear? Did you sleep?

GEORGES:     Not very well, Maman. I'm feeling rather weak.

HUGON:       I hope you're not coming down with something.

MUFFAT:      *Mea culpa, mea culpa, mea maxima culpa.*

HUGON:       Georges! What's that dreadful red mark on your neck?

GEORGES:     What? Oh it's nothing . . . an insect. I think I'll go for
a walk.

HUGON:       Do dear. *(Calls after him.)* Take Estelle with you. *(To
her, apologetic.)* He's not himself.

ESTELLE:     It's quite all right, Madame.

DAGUENET:    *(Coming over to her.)* Perhaps Mademoiselle will come
for a walk with me.

ESTELLE:     Oh no thank you, I –

HUGON:       What a good idea.

SABINE:      How very kind. Run along, dear.

*Estelle unwillingly takes Daguenet's arm and they go
off.*

FAUCHERY:    And perhaps Madame will come for a walk with me.

SABINE:      *(After a brief pause.)* Yes.

*They go. Muffat is alone on the stage, kneeling.*

MUFFAT: Lord I am not worthy that thou should enter under my roof – *(Breaks off. Begins to sway on his knees. His face turned up, eyes closed, an ecstatic chant. Music fades.)* Enter! Oh let me enter the temple of her body . . . my face between her breasts, her yellow hair wound around my nakedness. . . . With my body I thee worship, thy flesh is my refuge, thy mouth my joy and my salvation. Enter! Let me enter thy sweet secret paradise and be filled with rapture and heavenly delights. Embrace me! Enfold me! Possess me! Oh pour out the riches of thy body and wash me in the waters of thy glory. *(Beatific)* Nana! Nana! Nana! *(He opens his eyes and stares out front in an expression of horror. Buries his face in his hands, shuddering. After a moment he prays in a low, steady voice. Music.)* Lord I am not worthy that thou shouldst enter under my roof. Say but the word and my soul shall be healed.

> *Music fades out. He remains praying in silence. Nana comes on followed by Steiner. Zoe stands watching. Nana is carrying the Louis doll.*

STEINER: *(Petulant)* Well, why not?

NANA: I've already told you. I'm indisposed.

STEINER: What's wrong with you?

NANA: *(Gentle reproof.)* Really, Monsieur Steiner . . . *(Embarrassed and bad-tempered he goes off.)* Don't say it, Zoe. *(Ecstatic)* I'm in love! I love him. I'm happy.

ZOE: Well, Monsieur Steiner isn't.

NANA: I won't be unfaithful to my Zizi. *(Babytalk to doll.)* Will I, darling? Not to your new little Papa. No no no.

ZOE: Monsieur Steiner bought you this house!

NANA: Well it's mine now and Zizi and Baby and I are going to live here together forever and ever.

ZOE: And how is he going to keep you?

NANA: We're going to be country people and live off the land.

ZOE: Fairy tales! And what about your future? Your career?

NANA: I'm not listening, I'm not listening, I'm not listening.

*She dances up to meet Georges who comes on to her.*
*Annoyed, Zoe goes off. Estelle and Daguenet come on.*

ESTELLE:        *(Very shy.)* Are you acquainted with this actress,
                Monsieur Daguenet?

DAGUENET:       Who? Oh no. Never met her.

                *Music. Nana and Georges play ring a ring a rosy with*
                *the doll. They sing.*

MUFFAT:         Lamb of God who takest away the sins of the world
                have mercy on us. Lamb of God who takest away the
                sins of the world have mercy on us. Lamb of God who
                takest away the sins of the world grant us peace.

                *Music out. Nana and Georges who have been singing*
                *softly throughout the above now sink down on the*
                *floor. She holds the doll up to him.*

NANA:           Kiss Baby. *(He does. They look at each other.)* Oh I
                love you!

                *He kisses her and they lie with their arms around each*
                *other. Sabine and Fauchery come on.*

SABINE:         Monsieur Fauchery! I mustn't listen to you.

                *Then she laughs with pleasure.*

FAUCHERY:       This mole at the corner of your mouth. It's bewitching.

                *He kisses her. They walk slowly off together. Music.*

MUFFAT:         *(As they go.)* May thy body Oh Lord, of which I have
                eaten and thy blood of which I have drunk cleave to
                my inmost parts and no stain of sin remain in me.

                *He rises, crosses himself and goes off looking drained*
                *and peaceful. Music out.*

MATHILDE:       *(Offstage)* Nana! Nana, where are you?

FERNANDE:       *(Offstage)* We've arrived, Nana.

                *They come running on. Nana and Georges jump up.*

NANA:           Mathilde! Fernande! What are you doing here?

MATHILDE:       Come for the weekend like we promised.

FERNANDE:       She's forgotten she invited us. Labordette brought us
                down.

LABORDETTE: *(Coming in.)* Hello, dear child. Well I've brought the girls to see you. I thought you might be getting bored. *(A benign glance at Georges.)* But I see I was mistaken.

MATHILDE: How are you? How's the country?

FERNANDE: Homesick for Paris yet?

NANA: Not one tiny bit. I adore it here.

MATHILDE: Well, Bordenave says you can stay away as long as you like. He's got Louise Violaine to take over Venus.

FERNANDE: The crowds go mad over her. *(Annoyed, Nana goes and puts the doll down.)* Where's Steiner, by the way?

NANA: He had to go to Paris. He won't be back 'til tonight.

FERNANDE: Oh how convenient, eh Georgie?

NANA: *(Annoyed)* Mind your own business, Fernande.

LABORDETTE: Fine house, Nana.

MATHILDE: How many bedrooms?

NANA: Ten!

MATHILDE: Blimey!

FERNANDE: I'd get lost in a place this big.

LABORDETTE: Well I think it's charming. And the countryside is quite delightful. Why don't you take the girls on an outing, Nana?

NANA: Why not? *(Grand)* A champagne picnic on the river. *(They all go off. Georges sits holding the doll. Nana comes back.)* You'll come too won't you, Georges?

GEORGES: I can't. How can I? I mustn't be seen in public with you. My mother . . .

NANA: *(Tragic)* You don't love me. You're ashamed of me.

GEORGES: Of course I'm not. Don't cry, Nana. I do love you. I do.

NANA: Will you come then?

GEORGES: Yes.

*They go off. Madame Hugon, Fauchery, Daguenet and Sabine come on. Muffat comes on to meet them.*

HUGON: We thought we'd go as far as the river. It's such a charming walk.

*Sabine and Fauchery walk on ahead.*

MUFFAT: I'm afraid I must go back to Paris today, Madame. Something urgent.

HUGON: Oh I am sorry. Must you really leave today?

MUFFAT: *(Very calm.)* Yes. I must go.

HUGON: And poor Georges has had to go and see the doctor. These dreadful headaches.

*Sabine and Fauchery stop walking upstage.*

HUGON: Why aren't they going over the bridge? Why are they stopping? *(Nana and the girls and Georges come on as in a carriage.)* It's that dreadful woman!

*All the members of her party turn their backs on the carriage except Muffat who stands transfixed.*

GEORGES: *(Horror)* My mother!

*He stares straight ahead as they go past them and off.*

NANA: *(Furious)* Fine Gentlemen! Oh very polite! Can't even raise their fucking hats to ladies. Your mother turning her back on me. All of them . . . treating me like a leper!

HUGON: *(Looks after them. Screams)* It's Georges! With her! Oh my God . . . my God . . .

*She bursts into tears. Fauchery and Sabine lead her off.*

MUFFAT: *(Intense passion.)* That boy! She prefers that boy to me!

*He goes off. Nana comes on carrying the doll. It's evening at her house. She sits, looking grave and thoughtful. Mathilde and Fernande come on.*

MATHILDE: Where's Georgie got to, Nana?

NANA: I sent him home to apologise to his mother.

FERNANDE: *(Laughs)* Poor little bastard.

MATHILDE: Well he wasn't much fun today.

FERNANDE: Boring. I don't think much of country life, I must say. There's nothing to do.

STEINER: *(Coming in.)* Aren't you girls coming in to supper?

MATHILDE: Oh yes. I'm starving.

FERNANDE: Come on, Nana.

NANA: I don't want any supper.

STEINER: What? Don't want any supper?

MATHILDE: Oh leave her. She's been in a horrible mood all day.

*They go.*

NANA: I shall have you educated by the Jesuits, my little son. You'll be a gentlemen.

ZOE: *(Coming in.)* Monsieur le Comte Muffat de Beuville.

NANA: *(Hands her the doll in silence.)* Ask him to come in.

*Muffat comes on. Venot follows at a distance. Music.*

MUFFAT: *(To Venot.)* Leave me.

*Venot goes. Muffat and Nana stand in silence looking at each other. Then she goes slowly toward him. He almost falls on her in a passionate embrace and sinks down to the floor. As the music of the cancan gets very loud, Nana performs a fierce and wild cancan over the body of the Count.*

*END OF ACT ONE*

# ACT TWO

*Music. During the introduction the men have gathered at the back and are watching and catcalling at the women who are strolling about, chatting to each other, smoking, looking out at the audience etc. This should give the impression of a cheap dance hall. The cancan music starts and the women dance a ferocious cancan with the men whistling and shouting as they watch. Then the men join in, embracing the women, dancing with them, catching them as they cartwheel etc. The actress playing Nana ends up in a rather prim little dance with the actor playing Steiner. As the rest of the company goes noisily off, the actor playing Muffat carries on a chair and sits on it, the mirrored screen is set up and Nana breaks angrily away from Steiner.*

NANA:    *(Shouts)* My God, Steiner! What am I . . . some kind of cheap tart? If you don't have any money then get out. Or do you think you can have it for nothing. You don't suck the end of my finger without paying for it!

STEINER:    But Nana, I sold my iron works to buy you that house.

NANA:    So?

STEINER:    I've cashed in all my investments to pay your expenses. Everything I owned, Nana! I've borrowed money I can't repay. I've been declared a bankrupt, Nana!

NANA:    Well what do you expect me to do with a bankrupt! I need three thousand francs now, Steiner! And if you haven't got it, Steiner, then go away and leave me alone.

STEINER:    I'll get it. I swear I'll get it.

NANA:    Well don't bloody well come back till you do.

    *Steiner goes off. Nana moves up toward the mirrored screen. Muffat gets up and goes to her.*

MUFFAT:    *(Anticipation and pleasure.)* Nana . . .

NANA:    You're not staying tonight. I'm too tired.

MUFFAT:    But you promised.

NANA:      No I didn't. I said we'd see. Tomorrow morning, precious, all right?

MUFFAT:    *(Aroused)* Now. I want you now.

NANA:      *(Sharp)* No! In the morning. Go home now, dearest.

MUFFAT:    Don't send me away Nana, please. Please.

NANA:      Oh really. You're just like a little baby. All right, you can stay for a little while. *(Hands him newspaper.)* There's an article in here by Fauchery. Somebody told me it's all about me. You can read it while I get ready for bed.

> *Muffat takes the paper and goes to sit down. In front of the mirror Nana performs a dreamy narcissistic exercise examining herself with the depraved curiosity of a child, undulating her body, stroking parts of herself, craning to see her buttocks, kissing her own shoulder, squeezing her breasts in her hands and smiling with pleasure and a kind of naive admiration and fascination with her own beauty.*

MUFFAT:    *(Reads)* In this city lives a beautiful golden haired woman, risen from the lowest of the low. Born into bestial poverty, she has become a force of nature and avenges the stinking and seething masses of which she is the product. The fermenting misery of the pauper class has risen to the surface in her and now rots the aristocracy. She is the golden fly, the colour of sunshine, who has flown up out of the dung and now, buzzing, dancing and glittering is entering palaces through the windows and poisoning the men inside simply by alighting on them.

> *He lets the paper fall on the floor and watches Nana in her ecstasy of self-admiration with a kind of horror. Suddenly he gets up and seizes her, throws her on the floor and hurls himself on top of her.*

NANA:      *(As they struggle.)* Stop it! Stop it! You're hurting me! *(Then as she manages to extricate herself, rage.)* Is that how you make love to your wife?

MUFFAT:    Don't speak of her! You know nothing about decent women.

NANA: Decent! They aren't even clean. Not one of them would dare to show herself like this. Oh yes! I know all about decent women and their dirty little secrets.

MUFFAT: Hold your tongue!

NANA: I won't. Why should I? Tell me, what would you do if your wife was unfaithful?

MUFFAT: Be quiet! My wife is a good, respectable Christian woman.

NANA: Oh yes. She's like all the *ladies* isn't she. So grand. So far above me. *(Vicious)* So respectable she's having an affair with Fauchery.

MUFFAT: *(Aghast)* What are you talking about?

NANA: I'm talking about Fauchery making love to your wife. Fucking your wife. Your good decent wife.

MUFFAT: No! It's not true!

NANA: Of course it's true. Everybody in Paris knows about it except you. You're a cuckold!

MUFFAT: *(Torment)* No no no!

NANA: *(Sulky)* I didn't want to tell you.

MUFFAT: My family! My name!

NANA: Well what about me? Do you think I want a cuckold for a lover? It's pathetic.

MUFFAT: Oh my God . . . my God . . .

NANA: *(Mimicking)* Oh my God, my God! Such a terrible tragedy. Well now you know she's no different from me! *(Steiner comes bursting in. Nana in fury.)* What are you doing here? How did you get in?

STEINER: *(Stammering)* My key . . .

NANA: Bastard! I told you to give it back.

STEINER: But I've got the money, Nana. I've got the three thousand francs. Look, Nana, look!

NANA: I don't want your stinking charity. This is what I think of your three thousand francs!

*She throws the money at him. It showers all over the floor. He kneels down to pick it up, still looking imploringly at her.*

STEINER:  But Nana . . . my love!

NANA:  *(Shouts)* What do you know about love, you pig! Nothing! Both of you! You don't know about anything except sticking it in! I'm sick of you. Coming here insulting me . . . treating me like a prostitute. You can both go to hell! I'm in love. I'm in love with a real man!

*Fanton rolls on from behind the screen, half-naked and wrapped in a sheet.*

FANTON:  *(Laughs)* Oh we've got company have we? Good evening, Gentlemen. Excuse my *déshabille*.

NANA:  *(Fondling him and kissing him.)* My Fanton, my lovely lover. Oh Fanton make love to me. I want you. And you two, get out! Get out and don't ever come back!

*They have been staring paralysed with astonishment. Now broken and submissive they go off. Nana and Fanton laugh and go off as Madame Lerat and Zoe come on. As they speak they fold up a quilt together.*

LERAT:  She'll be back, you'll see.

ZOE:  I might as well stay on here. The rent's paid up for the quarter. Do you know, I remember Madame Blanche once. Wild about a cab driver. Just like that Fanton. Vicious fellow. Face like a monkey's bum.

LERAT:  Well there you are. Most women can't resist that type if the truth be told. A man who'll fart right in their faces!

ZOE:  She's left most of her hats behind. Do you want them?

LERAT:  Yes. *(Pointing to quilt.)* Ugh. Look at that.

ZOE:  Funny, isn't it. So clean in herself.

LERAT:  Has he been round? The Count?

ZOE:  Every day. Behaving like a wild thing. But he's been snapped up now. By Madame Rose Mignon.

LERAT:      No! Well you can't blame him. Once a pig's had his
            snout in the trough, eh?

ZOE:        Not that he wouldn't come running back. Madame
            Nana's only got to whistle for him. If only she'd be
            sensible.

LERAT:      Well she's left a fine mess here.

ZOE:        Took everything she could carry. Most of it not paid
            for of course. All the creditors are back again.

LERAT:      Pack of hounds after the vixen. Still . . . don't you
            worry. She won't stick life with that Fanton for long.

            *Zoe nods and goes off carrying the quilt. Music.*
            *During the music the actress playing Madame Lerat is*
            *transformed into Nana by the rest of the company.*
            *Part of her costume is taken off her and her hat, her*
            *hair is tied back and when Nana stands in front of her*
            *Lerat/Nana is pushed through her legs and pulled*
            *through the other side. In the meantime three actors,*
            *Bosc, Gerard and Fanton have set up chairs downstage*
            *and watch this. Lerat/Nana comes down to them.*
            *Music out. This is now the sitting room of the little*
            *flat that Nana is living in with Fanton. Gerard and*
            *Bosc have come to dinner.*

GERARD:     Delicious supper, Nana.

NANA/
LERAT:      Thank you. Gerard. What did you think of my
            carbonnade?

GERARD:     First rate. Excellent.

BOSC:       You're as good a cook as you are an actress, Nana.

FANTON:     Ha!

GERARD:     When are you coming back to the theatre, Nana? We
            miss you. We're doing Fauchery's play. That journalist
            fellow. The Little Duchess, it's called.

FANTON:     Godawful play.

BOSC:       Terrible.

NANA/
LERAT:      Anyway I'm much too busy looking after my man.

BOSC:        That's right. And keeping this nice little nest cosy.

NANA/
LERAT:       It's small but we love it, don't we Precious?

FANTON:      Silly cow.

NANA/
LERAT:       Oh I can hear baby crying.

             *Goes off.*

BOSC:        What? Had a baby already?

GERARD:      That's a neat trick in three weeks.

FANTON:      She wouldn't leave that kid of hers behind.

NANA/
LERAT:       *(Coming on with doll.)* He's our baby now. Our own
             little Louis. Who knows? Perhaps we'll have a little
             brother or sister for him one day.

FANTON:      Not if I can help it! Any tricks like that, my girl, and
             I'll have you down to Old Mother Baba with her
             knitting needle before you can pull your drawers back
             up.

NANA/
LERAT:       Oh you're always teasing. Go to Papa, Louis.

FANTON:      That's right. He loves his Daddy don't he. Say Papa,
             then. Say Papa.

BOSC:        Pale little thing. Is he ill?

NANA/
LERAT:       Goodness no. *(Takes doll.)* He's bursting with health.

GERARD:      *(Gets up.)* Come on, Bosc. We'd better be off. You're a
             lucky man, Fanton.

BOSC:        Don't forget, Nana. There's a nice little part for you in
             that play.

NANA/
LERAT:       I think a woman's place is in the home.

FANTON:      A woman's place is on her back. Or on her belly with
             her bum stuck up in the air.

| NANA/ | |
|---|---|
| LERAT: | Isn't he awful. Come again soon. |
| BOSC: | Count on it. What? Lovely free grub? |
| GERARD: | *(Kisses Nana.)* Change your mind Nana. It's a good part. Geraldine. A soubrette. |
| FANTON: | Soubrette! Tart, you mean. Yes she might be able to manage that all right. |
| NANA/ LERAT: | Who's playing the duchess? |
| GERARD: | Rose Mignon. |
| NANA/ LERAT: | I could play that part. |
| FANTON: | You! |
| NANA/ LERAT: | You don't think I can act? |
| FANTON: | I know you can't act. |
| BOSC: | Oh oh, lovers' tiff. We'd best get out of the way. |
| GERARD: | *(As they go.)* Better not tell her about that singer, Fanton. |

*They go.*

| NANA/ LERAT: | What did he mean? What singer? *(He doesn't respond.)* Are you seeing some other woman? Well? Are you? |
|---|---|
| FANTON: | By Christ, I'm not having this! Believe dirty lies about me, would you? |
| NANA/ LERAT: | I'm sorry, darling. I knew it was a lie really. |
| FANTON: | I should bloody well think so. And what's the idea asking those two to supper anyway? Filling their faces at my expense. You waste too much money. |
| NANA/ LERAT: | Well it's my money too. |
| FANTON: | All right, so you put a bit in. But just you stop being so pissing . . . *(Slurred)* extravagant. |

NANA/
LERAT:        *(Laughs)* I think my lovey's had a drop too much.

FANTON:       *(Rage)* Who do you think you're calling a drunk? And
              how much of my money is left, eh? How much have
              you spent? Well I'll tell you! There's only seven
              thousand left out of seventeen! My savings, you bitch!

NANA/
LERAT:        My savings too. And look what you spend on drink.

FANTON:       *(Roars)* What? *(He has taken off one of his shoes and now
              he hits the chair and the floor violently time after time.
              This is a physical metaphor for his beating her and with
              each 'blow' she flinches and screams.)* One! I'm taking
              care of all the money from now on. Two! You can take
              that bastard brat back to your aunt tomorrow. Three! I
              see who I want when I want and where I want without
              any fucking nagging from you. Four!

              *A rain of violent rapid blows. She has been lying on
              the floor. Now leaps up hysterically laughing and
              crying but as the blows go on she screams in pain and
              falls into the arms of the actress playing Nana who has
              been watching from the back and now runs forward
              and catches her.*

FANTON:       I'm going to bed.

NANA/
LERAT:        *(Breaking from the other Nana's arms.)* Fanton! Fanton!

FANTON:       Well?

              *She crawls across the stage to him as she speaks.*

NANA/
LERAT:        Forgive me. Please forgive me. *(When she reaches him
              she puts her arms round his legs and drags herself up his
              body.)* Oh Fanton my love, my man. Kiss me. Kiss me.
              Make love to me. Please!

              *He picks her up and carries her off. Music: Street
              waltz. Night on the streets. The women as tarts
              walking the streets, the men propositioning them,
              picking them up. This activity goes on through the
              scene. Satin comes on. A drunk comes up to her.*

| DRUNK: | Are you free? |
|---|---|
| SATIN: | Not for you, creep. |
| DRUNK: | Who do you think you're calling a – |
| SATIN: | *(Violently)* Piss off! |
| DRUNK: | All right . . . all right . . . |

*Staggers off. Nana comes on looking rather shabby and tired.*

SATIN: Hey Nana, over here! *(As Nana joins her.)* You're looking a bit rough. Come on, we'll go down towards l'Opéra. *(Music changes to steet aria. They walk downstage right.)* That Fanton been beating you up again?

NANA: He knocked me right across the room last night. For nothing. Kicking me . . . punching me.

SATIN: And then did you go to bed?

NANA: He nearly killed me.

SATIN: But you do love him don't you, Nana.

NANA: Oh God, Satin, I'm crazy about him.

SATIN: Don't I know! I had a boyfriend like that once. Used to leave me for dead on the floor. What a man he was!

NANA: Fanton's supposed to leave me three francs a day for the marketing. Not a sou today. *(Looking round at the passing men.)* One's enough tonight.

SATIN: *(Moving on.)* Nothing much worth picking up around here.

NANA: *(Follows her.)* I went to see La Tricon today. Told her I could be free in the afternoons. *(Angry)* She didn't want me.

SATIN: You're always better off working for yourself.

NANA: Do you know what she said to me? 'My clients are all very particular'!

SATIN: Particular . . . bitch. Take it from me, Nana, the richer they are the more obscene they are. Christ! Some of the things they ask you to do . . . sometimes they scare me! *(Moving on again.)* Come on.

WOMAN:     *(Seeing her.)* Hey Satin!

           *Music changes to street polka.*

SATIN:     Hey angel! Howgedow's tragedade togodonighgedight?

WOMAN:     Ogedoh kaygeday. Trygedy Bougedoule Migediche.

SATIN:     Toogedoo fargedar. Nogodo tigedime.

WOMAN:     Nogodot mugeduch rougedound hegedere.

SATIN:     Wegadill seegedee. Bye bye, sweetheart.

           *They kiss each other on the mouth and caress each
           others' bodies, then break away and laugh. The woman
           goes off.*

WOMAN:     *(Waving)* Bygedy bygedy.

NANA:      *(Disgusted)* What was all that?

SATIN:     Just brothel jabber.

NANA:      I don't mean that. Why did you kiss her like that?

           *Music fades out.*

SATIN:     *(Surprised)* Why not? We've been to bed together
           enough times. I'm nuts about her.

NANA:      I think that's disgusting.

SATIN:     Ever tried it?

NANA:      No and never will either.

SATIN:     Well it's a lot better than some of the garbage you fuck.

NANA:      That's business.

SATIN:     Exactly. And this isn't. *(Kisses her neck.)* This is fun.

NANA:      *(Pulls away, prim.)* Don't Satin. I don't like it.

SATIN:     Look out! There's police down there.

NANA:      Oh Jesus! Quick! Quick!

           *Starts to run.*

SATIN:     Don't run. Walk. Just walk.

           *She goes off. Nana tries not to run. Bumps into
           Gerard.*

GERARD:     Nana! What's the matter with you?

NANA:       *(Tense)* Police. Back there. Walk with me, Gerard.

GERARD:     Oh I see. Back on the market, eh? *(Caresses her.)* Come up to my rooms, then.

NANA:       No!

GERARD:     If you're selling it, what's wrong with me?

NANA:       *(Outrage)* One of Fanton's friends? I'd rather starve!

GERARD:     Very touching. Well I'm not going your way, darling. You'll have to look after yourself.

            *He goes.*

NANA:       Bastard!

            *Goes off trying not to run. Satin comes on with the Marquis de Chouard just behind her.*

SATIN:      All right, I heard you. Fifty francs.

CHOUARD:    Oh yes! Yes yes yes. fifty francs. Yes!

SATIN:      And anything extra's twenty more. Got that?

CHOUARD:    Understood. Understood. Yes yes yes. *(Fondles her)*.

SATIN:      Not in the street for Christ's sake!

            *She walks away from him and into her room. He follows bent nearly double with excitement. She holds out her hand. He takes bills from his pocket and, taking hold of her head, pushes them into her mouth. She pulls them out. Sits on the floor.*

SATIN:      Want it straight? *(Spreads her legs.)* Bet you don't.

CHOUARD:    *(Kneeling beside her.)* How old are you child, eh? Eh?

SATIN:      Sixteen and a half and I'm not a child, you slimy old slug.

CHOUARD:    Sixteen and a half! That's nice, oh that's nice. Yes yes yes! *(Sniffs the air.)* Oh this is a dirty room. Oh yes, lovely stink, lovely stink. *(Nuzzling her.)* Oh smelly! Dirty! *(Pleasure)* Rancid . . .

SATIN:      Thanks. *(He buries his face in her clothes, snuffling. Satin in contempt.)* Oh God.

*He takes hold of one of her feet.*

CHOUARD: Shoes! Nice nice. Can I take your shoes off? Say yes! Say yes!

SATIN: *(Bored)* Yes.

CHOUARD: *(Taking a shoe off.)* Can Daddy borrow your shoe just for a minute? Can Daddy have little baby girl's shoes? Eh? Eh? Say yes!

SATIN: Yes.

*He forces her up on her feet, pushes one of her feet into his groin and, holding the shoe over his face, starts to buck and writhe. She looks at him with disgust. Looks away.*

CHOUARD: *(Takes the shoe off his face.)* Watch me! Watch me!

SATIN: *(Holds out her hand.)* That's extra.

CHOUARD: *(Urgent. Gets out money.)* Yes yes yes! A hundred francs. A hundred. Watch me!

*Satin puts her hands on her hips and looks at him.*

SATIN: Off you go then, Daddy dear.

*He puts the shoe back up to his face and sniffing and grunting for a few moments, cries out as he achieves a shuddering climax. Satin grabs her shoe and sits down on the floor as he lies sprawled and spent. Nana enters and runs across to the other side of the stage. Knocks on a screen. She is watched by a little group of neighbours.*

NANA: Fanton! Let me in! It's Nana.

*Knocks again.*

WOMAN: Bolted the door has he, dearie?

NANA: None of your business! *(Knocks again.)* Fanton!

MAN: He's in there. You can see the light under the door.

NANA: *(Knocking)* Let me in!

OTHERS: (Mocking) Let me in! Let me in!

NANA: *(Still knocking.)* Fanton!

*Stops knocking.*

FANTON:     *(From inside.)* Piss off!

            *Nana stands stock still for a moment from shock. Then
            starts to knock desperately again on the door.*

MAN:        She'll have that door down.

NANA:       *(Still knocking.)* Fanton! Fanton!

FANTON:     *(From inside.)* Piss off!

NANA:       Let me in! *(Fanton appears with a woman behind him.
            They are both in a state of partial undress. The
            neighbours jeer and catcall and laugh.)* Fanton!

            *Goes towards him. He pushes her away.*

FANTON:     God almighty, haven't you done yet? What do you
            want? Can't you let us get some sleep, you noisy bitch?
            *(Nana starts to cry.)* Clear off or I'll wring your neck!

            *Music. Nana runs off to the laughter of the crowd. She
            crosses the stage weeping to Satin's room.*

SATIN:      *(To Chouard.)* Now get out of here you dirty old piece
            of shit. Marquis of Muck, you are.

            *He seizes her hair and pulls himself up to his feet.
            Shuffles out, buttoning his clothes.*

NANA:       Satin! Satin! *(Bumps into Chouard.)* Oh my God, who's
            that!

CHOUARD:    *(Hiding his face.)* Nobody. Nobody.

NANA:       Oh Satin, he's locked me out!

SATIN:      Fanton? Oh the bastard. Don't cry, Nana. Don't cry.

NANA:       *(Sobbing)* She was there! That stinking ugly little singer
            with half her clothes off. I'll kill her! And I'll kill him
            too!

            *Music fades out.*

SATIN:      *(Embracing her.)* Never mind, you're silly to get in such
            a state. I'm here and I love you.

NANA:       Oh Satin, how could he treat me like that?

SATIN:      *(Caressing her.)* It's what they do. Dirty swine, all of
            them.

NANA:       I love him so much. I was so good to him. Oh my
            beautiful Fanton!

SATIN:      Forget him. We won't have anything more to do with
            men you and me, eh?

            *She kisses Nana on the mouth. Nana responds. Then
            she laughs with pleasure and the two of them roll over
            and lie on the floor murmuring, kissing and laughing.
            Suddenly a loud knocking from outside. Satin sits
            upright. The knocking goes on.*

SATIN:      Christ! It's the police!

NANA:       *(Terrified)* How do you know? How do you know it is?

SATIN:      I always do know. Shit! This'll mean a night in jail.

NANA:       *(Panic)* I can't! Satin I can't! I couldn't bear it! I'm
            getting out! *(She runs wildly across the stage and knocks
            on a different screen)* Auntie, let me in. It's Nana.

LERAT:      *(Appearing round the screen.)* There. I knew you'd come
            back.

            *Sabine and Fauchery enter and stand by the piano.
            Music. As it plays, Muffat comes on at a diagonal
            upstage in a top hat.*

MUFFAT:     *(Calls)* Sabine!

            *Sabine looks at him. Takes a few steps towards him.*

SABINE:     *(Polite)* Muffat. What a surprise.

MUFFAT:     I wanted to speak to you.

SABINE:     Did you? *(Courteous hostess.)* Are you coming in?
            *(Music comes up loud. The pianist and Fauchery laugh.
            Sabine smiles at Muffat.)* A few friends.

MUFFAT:     *(Desperate)* Sabine!

            *Music out.*

SABINE:     *(Amiable)* Yes?

MUFFAT:        *(Uncertain and halting at first.)* I realise I have been
               . . . to blame. *(Growing formal and rather pompous.)*
               However, I assure you it meant nothing. Nothing! An
               aberration. A kind of sickness. As Monsieur Venot says,
               it was a trial sent by God. But it is over. Finished. We
               must forget it ever happened. What is important now is
               our life together, our family name . . .

SABINE:        *(Friendly)* I'm afraid I don't follow you.

               *Music.*

MUFFAT:        *(Raising his voice over this.)* People have said that *you*
               . . . that you . . .

               *He can't go on.*

SABINE:        *(Smiling)* That I what?

MUFFAT:        Believe me I know that none of it is . . . I never never
               for a moment. . . . rumours, malicious gossip – lies!
               You of all women in the world . . . impossible! *(Music
               out. Muffat intensely:)* Not true, I know that Sabine.
               Not true!

               *He looks at her imploringly. She returns his look
               calmly. Fauchery comes up and puts his arm around
               her. Muffat drops his eyes and turns heavily away.
               Fauchery and Sabine stroll back towards the piano and
               off. The rest of the company comes on. It is a rehearsal
               at the Théâtre des Variétés. Muffat walks blindly
               through them. Nobody takes any notice of him. All
               actors have scripts except Rose. Fauchery sits at the
               side watching and following in the script.*

BORDENAVE:     All right. Get going. What's the hold-up? Act two,
               scene six. Get on, Mathilde you stupid bitch.

MATHILDE:      Sorry, Bordenave. It's so cold in here my brain's
               frozen.

BORDENAVE:     Well, act! Act! That'll warm you up.

MATHILDE:      Where did you say the door's going to be?

BORDENAVE:     Jesus! How many times? There are chalk marks
               upstage!

MATHILDE:      Oh yes. *(Mimes throwing open doors.)* Madame la
               Duchesse!

ROSE:        *(Comes on with great panache.)* Baron d'Alençon! Here already.

FANTON:      *(Reads)* My dear, I didn't think you would come.

ROSE:        I said I would, Monsieur, and I'm not in the habit of breaking my word. Besides I was curious. I've never been in the house of a courtesan before.

             *Fernande and Simonne are sitting at the side chatting and giggling.*

BORDENAVE:   *(To them.)* Shut up!

FANTON:      If your family hears of this visit they may be angry.

ROSE:        They may.

FANTON:      Ah! *(Takes her arm.)* May I present my nephew Alphonse Tardiveau and his friends –

ACTOR:       Enchanted, Madame la Duchesse. What a great pleasure it is to –

FANTON:      Just a minute. Where are the friends?

BORDENAVE:   Mime them. Mime them. I'm getting in extras for those parts. They hardly speak.

FAUCHERY:    Some of them do. There's the section where they discuss the court and –

BORDENAVE:   We can cut all that. *(As Fauchery starts to protest.)* Is Nana here?

             *He speaks so only Fauchery can hear.*

FAUCHERY:    Yes. In a first tier box. I told you. Labordette's fixed a meeting between her and Muffat.

BORDENAVE:   Is he going to back the show?

FAUCHERY:    Yes, if she takes the part of Geraldine.

BORDENAVE:   She'll take it. So where's the Count?

FAUCHERY:    In the Prop Room.

BORDENAVE:   Right. *(To company.)* Top of page forty-six. "Really this is the most enchanting evening" . . . Rose?

ROSE:        Really, this is the most enchanting evening I've had this season. Heavens! What a lot of peculiar people!

FAUCHERY :        *(Goes to her.)* Out front, Rose, out front! It's a laugh
                  line. At the audience. "Really this is the most
                  enchanting evening I've had this season. . . ." *(Turns to
                  face out.)* "Heavens what a lot of peculiar people!"

ROSE :            *(Affronted, to Bordenave.)* And then straight upstage to
                  Geraldine?

BORDENAVE :  Right.

ROSE :            *(Exasperated)* Well, where is she?

BORDENAVE :  Old Bosc's reading her in. Bosc! Where the devil are
                  you? *(To Rose.)* Geraldine's not cast yet. Come on,
                  Bosc. You're supposed to be on the Baron's lap here.

                  *Bosc has shuffled on, a cigarette dangling from his lips
                  and holding his script.*

ROSE :            I thought Simonne was playing Geraldine.

BORDENAVE :  Well she's not. It's far too good a part for Simonne.
                  Too difficult. Geraldine's really the most important
                  part in the play.

ROSE :            *(Angry)* What do you mean, the most –

BORDENAVE :  All right, Rose, all right. Carry on, Bosc.

BOSC :            *(On Fanton's lap, reads.)* Won't your wife Madame la
                  Baronne, be angry if –

BORDENAVE :  Hang on. It's no good having that speech there,
                  Fauchery. It gives away the end of the act. Better cut
                  straight through to the kiss.

                  *Fauchery starts to rise angrily, then subsides.*

BORDENAVE :  *(To actors.)* All right. We're cutting down to the
                  bottom of page forty-seven. The kiss now, Bosc. Good
                  and loud.

                  *Bosc takes his cigarette out of his mouth and kisses
                  Fanton smackingly on the cheek.*

FANTON :          God . . . your breath!

BOSC :            *(Ignores this.)* Oh Monsieur Baron, you've made me the
                  happiest girl in the world!

ROSE: Kissing in public! What a way to behave. *(Aside)* But it seems to have brought this Geraldine success. With men and with money!

FERNANDE: Go on, Simonne. It's you!

SIMONNE: Oh Christ! *(Runs on to acting area.)* Madame la Duchesse, I followed your carriage here and –

BORDENAVE: Late! Late! Late!

SIMONNE: Ow! Sorry Bordenave.

BORDENAVE: Stupid cow. All right. We'll break here. Tomorrow at ten.

BOSC: What? Letting us off early?

FANTON: Come on, quick. Before he changes his mind.

*All the actors go except Rose.*

BORDENAVE: Bloody actors.

FAUCHERY: Never mind, you'll soon have your money.

BORDENAVE: *(Going off.)* Let's go and wait for him upstairs.

ROSE: Wait for who?

FAUCHERY: Some backer.

ROSE: How's the Countess Muffat de Beuville these days?

FAUCHERY: Awfully well, thanks.

*Music. A screen is set up downstage to represent the prop room. Now the whole company come onto the stage from various directions. They are all playing Nana briefly and each speaks one of her lines from earlier in the play. The actress playing Nana stands at the side of the screen watching. At some point Fauchery and Muffat come on to the area in front of the screen and stand looking at each other. The actor playing Fauchery is now Nana.*

1: I'm in love with a real man!

2: When I get home tonight I can go to bed all by myself.

3: Fucking vultures I hate them.

4: Will you come then?

5:              I need three thousand francs now!

6:              Treating me like a prostitute!

7:              Oh they're so juicy!

ALL:            *(Plus Fauchery.)* Well?

NANA/
FAUCHERY:       *(Going on immediately.)* We didn't come here to stand
                looking at each other like a pair of china dogs, did we?

MUFFAT:         *(Goes to her.)* Oh Nana . . .

NANA/
FAUCHERY:       Look, there was wrong on both sides and I'm ready to
                forgive you, so let's shake hands and be good friends.

MUFFAT:         Good friends?

NANA/
FAUCHERY:       Why not?

MUFFAT:         I don't want that. I've come to take you back. I want
                to begin again.

NANA/
FAUCHERY:       *(Grave)* Oh that's impossible, my dear.

MUFFAT:         Why?

NANA/
FAUCHERY:       *(Calm)* Because I don't want to.

MUFFAT:         Don't say that! Listen – I've seen a house in the Parc
                Monceau. It's yours! I'll make you the richest woman
                in Paris. Servants, carriages, furs, diamonds – anything
                you want! I'll furnish your house like a palace. My only
                condition is you'll be mine alone. No one else. My
                whole fortune, Nana! All for you!

NANA/
FAUCHERY:       Have you finished pawing me? The answer is no. No.
                No. No. It's funny how rich men think they can get
                anything with their money. A woman could die in one
                of your bloody palaces if she didn't have love.

MUFFAT:         But I love you! I do!

NANA/
FAUCHERY:   I know of something that's worth more than money.
            *(With feeling.)* Oh, if only someone would give me
            what I long for. *(He looks up with hope.)* You? You
            wouldn't understand.

            *Muffat buries his face in his hands. When he looks up
            it is with astonishment to see Fauchery/Nana giving
            his version of the Duchess in the play. He minces round
            the room, strutting like a portly hen afraid of dirtying its
            claws, fluttering his lashes, swaying his hips, looking
            through an imaginary lorgnette etc. Muffat watches,
            utterly confused.*

NANA/
FAUCHERY:   *(Very affected voice.)* I'm not in the habit of breaking
            my word, you know. Besides I was curious. I've never
            been in the house of a courtesan. *(To Muffat.)* What do
            you think?

MUFFAT:     *(Dazed)* What are you doing?

NANA/
FAUCHERY:   The part of the Duchess in the play! If they think I'm
            going to play that tart! *(Back into performance.)* Kissing
            in public! What a way to behave! But if seems to have
            brought this Geraldine success. With men and with
            money! *(Stops, triumphant.)* That's it, isn't it!

MUFFAT:     *(Stammering)* Oh . . . absolutely . . . yes . . . that's it!

NANA/
FAUCHERY:   *(Modest)* I've been practicing. *(Passionate)* I've got to
            have that part do you understand? *(Soft, pleading.)*
            Will you get it for me, darling?

MUFFAT:     I? But that's impossible.

NANA/
FAUCHERY:   *(Impatient)* Just go and tell them you want me to play
            it. They need your money.

MUFFAT:     *(Anguish)* I can't ask that . . . *(Gets the name out with
            painful difficulty.)* Fauchery . . . for a favour!

NANA/
FAUCHERY:   *(Unpleasant)* But in the circumstances, my dear, how
            could he possibly refuse you?

MUFFAT:        Don't! I can't! Don't make me do that!

                    *A pause. Nana/Fauchery takes Muffat's face in his*
                    *hands.*

NANA/
FAUCHERY:      Do it and I'll let you buy me that big house. Yes! I'll
               be yours. Yours alone! (*Kisses him passionately on the*
               *lips.*) Go!

                    *Muffat reels out of the room. He meets Bordenave*
                    *downstage and now the actor playing Fauchery returns*
                    *to character.*

BORDENAVE:     (*Fulsome*) Count Moffat. How delightful to see you.
               You know our author of course, Monsieur Fauchery.

MUFFAT:        (*Not looking at Fauchery.*) Nana wants the part of the
               Duchess.

FAUCHERY:      What!

BORDENAVE:     But that's mad!

                    *Fanton has come on unseen by the others during the*
                    *above and after listening, goes off again.*

MUFFAT:        (*Rapid, excitable.*) No no, not mad, I assure you. She's
               just been showing me how she'd play it. Perfect! Such
               distinction! Like this, you see. Like this. (*To their*
               *amazement he begins mincing round the room in an*
               *imitation of Nana's performance as the Duchess. Sways*
               *his hips, makes the same grotesque gestures, gets out*
               *fragments of the speech.*) Not in the habit of breaking
               my word . . . curious . . . never been in a courtesan's
               house . . . kissing in public! . . . brought this Geraldine
               success with men and with money! . . . (*Stops;*
               *pleadingly to Bordenave.*) You see? You see?

                    *Bordenave stares at him, trying not to laugh, and nods*
                    *energetically.*

FAUCHERY:      I'm sorry. It's impossible. The part has been given to
               Rose Mignon.

                    *Fanton has come back on with Rose. They stand at the side*
                    *and listen.*

BORDENAVE:     Oh well . . . I can fix that.

FAUCHERY: No! Definitely not!

MUFFAT: *(Finally looks at him, Speaks falteringly.)* I ask this as a favour.

FAUCHERY: Not possible.

MUFFAT: I beg you. *(Pause, his voice hard.)* I insist.

FAUCHERY: *(Defeated.)* Well of course . . . if she really wants it . . . of course!

ROSE: *(Coming to them enraged.)* If *she* wants it! It's my part! *(Looks at Muffat. He turns away. She turns to the others.)* How dare you! My husband will sue you for breaking my contract, Bordenave.

FAUCHERY: *(Uncomfortable)* Now now, Rose . . .

ROSE: You bastard! I won't have this.

BORDENAVE: Yes you will. It's all been settled.

ROSE: *(Hatred)* You're despicable. All of you! Despicable!

> *She goes out.*

NANA: *(Shouts from upstage.)* Well? Do I get the part?

> *Music. All the men run to her and sit in a line in front of her, gazing hungrily up at her while she laughs. The music becomes the cancan and, just as the women did at the beginning of the act, the men dance the cancan with the women looking on, shouting and laughing and jeering. Toward the end of the dance the men take money out of their pockets and throw it up in the air and shout "Money! Money! Money!" Their dance ends with them turning their backs, bending over with their bottoms thrust out. There is a loud discordant chord from the music which seems to propel the whole company off the stage. The chord is held while a chair is brought on. Two of the actors come on as footmen, Nana swirls on wearing jewels and sits on the chair. Georges has run on with her carrying the doll and he sits at her feet almost inside her skirts. Muffat stands across from Nana. We should get the impression of a big room. This is Nana's new house in the Parc Monceau. Satin comes on smoking. Music fades out.*

NANA:          *(Angry to Satin.)* Where have you been? *(Pause)* Well?
               Answer me! *(Satin doesn't bother to answer or look at
               her.)* Two days! You've been gone for two days. Where
               were you? What were you doing? Who were you with?

SATIN:         I can't remember. It doesn't matter.

NANA:          It matters to me! Did I bring you here to live in my
               house and buy you new clothes so you could go
               running around after other women. *(Melodrama)* Or
               have you been out on the streets again . . . picking up
               men!

SATIN:         Oh leave it out, Nana. Just because the rest of Paris is
               going wild about you, don't think you can pull the
               duchess on me. *(Laughs)* You made enough of a mess of
               it in the theatre. Booed off the stage.

GEORGES:       She was wonderful. She was stupendous.

NANA:          *(Emotional)* There! Georges loves me. Ran away from
               his mama just to be with me, didn't you baby.

GEORGES:       *(Like a parrot.)* I'll always love you, Nana.

               *She strokes him. He tries to embrace her but she ignores
               him.*

NANA:          *(To Satin.)* But you don't, do you. Go on, Say it. You
               don't love me any more.

GEORGES:       *(As before.)* I'll always love you, Nana.

SATIN:         *(Looking straight at Nana.)* You know I'm mad about
               you.

MUFFAT:        I won't have this, Nana! *(Looks at Satin. Looks away.)*
               This . . . this boy! All the men who come to this house
               . . .

NANA:          *(Outrage)* What? *(Seizes the doll from Georges.)* Didn't I
               swear a sacred oath on my child's head that I would be
               utterly and absolutely faithful to you?

MUFFAT:        *(Cowers)* Yes . . . yes . . .

               *Satin laughs.*

NANA:          Naturally I have friends, I entertain, visitors come to
               call. And Georges here is like a little brother to me.

GEORGES:     *(Trying to climb up inside her skirts.)* Take me to bed, Nana.

NANA:        *(Pushes him away, hardly aware of him.)* And you're surely not jealous of Satin!

SATIN:       *(Grins)* Surely not!

NANA:        *(Laughs)* What does it matter to you what we do? My girlfriend! *(Then grave.)* I think you should apologise to me, Count.

MUFFAT:      I do. I beg your pardon. Forgive me. *(Gets out a jeweller's box.)* And I have a little –

NANA:        *(To footman.)* Here. Take Baby and give him to my Aunt. *(Kisses doll.)* My little Louis . . . Ugh, what's this? He's got pus or something coming out of his ears. *(Smacks doll lovingly.)* Dirty boy. *(To footman.)* Tell my Aunt to clean out his ears.

             *Footman takes the doll and goes off.*

MUFFAT:      *(Going to Nana.)* Dearest . . . a surprise for –

SATIN:       Let's go out to a café to eat tonight, Nana.

NANA:        All right, if you want to.

SATIN:       We can get dressed up as men and pick up some girls.

             *They laugh.*

MUFFAT:      *(Trotting up to her again.)* Look Nana, I've brought –

GEORGES:     Don't go out, Nana. Don't leave me.

NANA:        *(Impatient)* Stop being such a nuisance, Georges.

             *Satin whispers into Nana's ear. She laughs delightedly. Muffat gets a necklace out of the box and holding it in one hand he stretches his two closed fists out to Nana.*

MUFFAT:      Which hand, Nana? Guess!

SATIN:       *(Scornful)* Oh, what's Daddy got?

MUFFAT:      Guess! Guess!

NANA:        In a minute! *(Confidential to Satin.)* Did I tell you? I've made him say Mimi can marry his daughter Estelle.

| | |
|---|---|
| SATIN: | *(Laughs)* What? Your old boyfriend? |
| NANA: | And Mimi's going to give me a commission. |
| SATIN: | How much? |
| NANA: | *(Giggles)* It isn't how much, it's what. |
| SATIN: | Well what then? |
| NANA: | None of your business, you dirty little cow. |

*She dances back to Muffat.*

| | |
|---|---|
| MUFFAT: | Which hand? Guess! Guess! |
| NANA: | That one. |
| MUFFAT: | *(Opens his hand, proud.)* Those sapphires you asked me to buy for you! |
| NANA: | Oh. *(Takes necklace.)* How funny. They don't look nearly as pretty as they did in the shop window. |
| MUFFAT: | *(Desolate)* But Nana, they cost – |

*Doorbell. Nana turns, surprised. Lets the necklace fall.*

| | |
|---|---|
| NANA: | Who can that be? |
| ZOE: | *(Coming in.)* Lieutenant Philippe Hugon. *(To Georges.)* Your brother! |
| GEORGES: | *(Panic)* He's come to fetch me home! Don't let him take me away from you, Nana! |
| NANA: | *(Haughty)* I'd like to see him try. Show him in. |

*Zoe goes, picking up the necklace and slipping it into her pocket. Philippe comes in and stands looking sternly at Nana after first bowing to the Count, clicking his heels.*

| | |
|---|---|
| PHILIPPE: | May I request a word with you alone, Madame? |
| NANA: | *(Smiles)* of course. Count? You don't mind? |
| MUFFAT: | Indeed not, my dear. *(To Georges.)* Come along, my boy. *(Leading Georges out.)* You should be grateful to your brother. It's high time you got back to your studies. |
| NANA: | *(Very seductive.)* What was it you wanted to speak to me about, Lieutenant? |

SATIN: *(Exasperated disgust.)* Oh Christ!

    *She goes.*

PHILIPPE: *(Great dignity.)* Madame, my mother is in a state of extreme distress about my young brother. I have come to insist . . . *(Nana comes up close to him. He walks away.)* . . . to . . . insist . . .

    *Nana has followed him. She looks him in the eyes and then strolls away but he seizes her by the hair and kisses her passionately. Music. He slides down her body, embracing her, eyes closed, ecstatic. As the music changes to the dada surrealist theme, Nana assumes the posture of a fly, arms outstretched with one hand touching Philippe and the other to land on one of the men. All the other men are coming rapidly toward her, they too with the jerky movements of flies. In the background the other women move about with the same kind of movement.*

NANA: Money! I need money! More! More!

MAN: I say . . . hang it all, Nana. You've had every penny of my fortune. There's only the family château left to sell.

NANA: Well sell it, silly.

    *Kisses him.*

MAN: *(Rapture)* Ruined by the most famous courtesan in Paris!

NANA: Get me money! Get it for me now!

PHILIPPE: I could borrow some from regimental funds.

NANA: Do it, darling! Do it just for me!

MUFFAT: *(Coming up.)* I'll sell my wife's land in Lyons.

NANA: Good boy!

    *Kisses him.*

MUFFAT: Promise you're not sleeping with anybody but me.

NANA: Oh I promise, pet, I promise! Steiner! You're back! Got any money?

STEINER: Made a killing on the stock market, Nana. Bought three armament factories.

NANA:          Sell them! Sell them! I want new horses!

MAN:           I've named one of my horses after you, Nana. She's
               entered in the Grand Prix.

MAN:           Come and see her run!

MAN:           See her run! See Nana run!

NANA:          We're going to the races! *(The other women come swiftly
               to join the group. One of them puts the doll up on Nana's
               shoulders.)* The races! The races!

                    *The music has changed to the loud sound of thundering
                    hooves. The group turns slowly as watching the race.
                    Nana has backed away and stands upstage and raised
                    up, watching. The actors say the following lines singly
                    with great urgency.*

               They're off! Where's Nana? There she is. Come on
               Nana. Come on Nana. She'll never do it. Come on
               Nana. Coming up fast. Come on Nana. She's winning!
               She's winning! She's winning! Come on Nana. Come
               on Nana. Come on Nana.

                    *Now they are all shouting her name (not in unison),
                    almost chanting it as they turn to face upstage to
                    Nana. She stands smiling and triumphant as they go
                    on chanting her name. A goddess and her
                    worshippers. . . . At a sudden discordant note she
                    doubles up in pain and falls onto the floor in a
                    crouched posture. The men draw back. Two of the
                    women lift Nana to a standing position while the
                    actress who plays Satin (and who will play Nana in
                    the next scene) moves downstage centre and another
                    holds her as she stands writhing in pain. The same
                    movement is echoed by Nana at the back. Then Nana
                    is brought downstage by the two women and
                    Satin/Nana sinks to the floor in front of her. The
                    upper part of her body is against Nana's legs. Nana
                    stands looking down at her throughout the scene. Four
                    of the men stand in the downstage area with their
                    backs turned to the two Nanas. Muffat goes up to the
                    side. Zoe comes downstage of the two Nanas and draws
                    out from under Satin/Nana a sheet heavily stained
                    with blood. She holds it up for a moment. Then she*

*hands it to one of the other women who takes it and
goes slowly offstage with the other woman. Zoe goes up
to Muffat as if letting him into Nana's bedroom.*

ZOE: Come in, Monsieur le Comte. Madame nearly died last night!

MUFFAT: *(Horrified)* What's wrong with her, Zoe? What is it?

ZOE: Something incredible, Monsieur. A miscarriage! *(At this the four other men slink off the stage.)* I found her this morning in a dead faint. In a pool of blood. As if if she'd been murdered!

MUFFAT: *(Aghast)* My God!

*He goes and sinks on his knees beside Satin/Nana.*

NANA/
SATIN: *(Very weak.)* Oh my sweet . . . I thought I would never see you again.

MUFFAT: Don't say that, Nana.

NANA/
SATIN: Will you forgive me? I was afraid to tell you. *(Weeps)* Our little child. Yours and mine.

MUFFAT: *(Almost in tears too.)* My brave girl!

NANA/
SATIN: There's something I want to say to you. Listen, dearest, you must go back to your wife.

MUFFAT: No! No!

NANA/
SATIN: Hush. You can still come here whenever you like. This is your house and I'm yours alone, you know that. but you must live at home now.

MUFFAT: I can't go back there!

NANA/
SATIN: We mustn't be selfish, dear. Your little daughter Estelle getting married . . . it's not fair to her . . .

*A cry of pain.*

MUFFAT: Please!

NANA/
SATIN:          *(Gentle)* You must be brave now too. I'm only thinking of what's best for you . . . your reputation.

MUFFAT:        *(Moved)* I know, I know. You're so good to me, Nana.

NANA/
SATIN:          Go now, my dear. I must rest. *(He kisses her and gets up.)* Will you do something for me, darling? Will you buy me a new bed? This one would always remind me of our tragedy.

MUFFAT:        Yes. Yes, of course I will.

NANA/
SATIN:          There's my dear generous love.

                *He tiptoes out. The two Nanas watch him go expressionlessly. Then Nana pulls Satin/Nana up to her feet.*

BOTH:           Whoever did give me the little bastard should have kept it to himself!

                *They do a sinuous rippling movement and Satin/Nana gets thrown off by Nana as if by a snake casting off its old skin.*

NANA:           *(Looking down at herself.)* Fancy my own body playing me a dirty trick like that! *(Daguenet comes in a flowing white scarf.)* Mimi! What are you doing here? And on your wedding day. What's the matter?

DAGUENET:       *(Solemn)* I've come to pay you my commission. *(Then he laughs.)* After the church service and before the wedding night, wasn't that the bargain?

NANA:           Yes it was, Mimi, it was!

                *She laughs. Music.*

                And you still smell of incense! *(They start to waltz.)* Fuck me then, Mimi, fuck me little bridegroom. Oh harder than that! Harder, Mimi, harder!

                *The rest of the company come on in couples and waltz round the stage. When the music suddenly becomes disonant they stop and stand looking uneasy and afraid, their bodies contorted. Then when the waltz begins again they resume dancing. Finally they all waltz off leaving Nana and Sabine standing, separately, alone on the stage. Music out.*

NANA:     I want the most beautiful bed in the world!

SABINE:   My house! I want it all redecorated. Every room!

NANA:     I want!

SABINE:   *(Overlapping eagerly.)* I want!

NANA:     Solid gold and silver. All hand done!

SABINE:   Velvet curtains lined in satin! Lace! Silk!

NANA:     I must have!

SABINE:   *(Overlapping)* I must have!

NANA:     Garlands of flowers carved along the sides.

SABINE:   Thick, soft carpets . . . pure cashmere rugs . . .

NANA:     Gold cupids dancing on a silver trellis.

SABINE:   A marble staircase, embroidered tapestries.

NANA:     I want . . . I want . . .

SABINE:   *(Overlapping)* I need . . . I need . . .

NANA:     A gold statue of me as the goddess of night.

SABINE:   Walls covered in silk . . . a fountain set with jewels . . .

NANA:     The goddess lying naked on mother of pearl clouds.

SABINE:   A mirror hanging in every room.

NANA:     I want . . . I've got to have . . . I need . . .

SABINE:   *(Overlapping)* I want . . . I've got to have . . . I need . . .

BOTH:     More . . . more . . . more . . . more.

*At this point the rest of the actors come on and drift restlessly round the stage all murmuring together but not in unison.*

ALL:      I want . . . I must have . . . I need . . . more . . . more . . . I've got to have . . . I need . . . I want . . . I want . . . I must have . . . I need . . . more . . . more . . . more . . . etc.

*The actor playing the Marquis de Chouard cuts across this, striding across the stage. Muffat tries to keep up behind him. Venot stands apart watching. The rest of the actors go off.*

CHOUARD:    No! No! No! No! No!

MUFFAT:    *(Pleads)* Only a small loan. Just for a few weeks. Please!

*He grabs hold of Chouard's arm who shakes him off.*

CHOUARD:    Don't touch me! I don't want anything to do with you. You've brought disgrace on us all. I'm sure Monsieur Venot agrees with me.

VENOT:    *(Coming up to him.)* Well well, my dear Marquis, we must forgive others must we not, if we wish to merit forgiveness ourselves.

CHOUARD:    *(Nonplussed)* I don't know what you mean. *(Then angry and self-righteous again.)* No! no! No! That kind of indulgence leads to the abyss. No. He's beyond forgiveness. *(Contempt)* He's the scandal of the court. It's intolerable! There's talk he may be asked to resign from the Chamber of Deputies.

MUFFAT:\    *(Imploring)* Just a small loan. Fifteen thousand. Ten.

CHOUARD:    *(Virulent)* Don't speak to me! The Empress herself has said you disgust her!

*He strides off. Venot goes towards Muffat.*

MUFFAT:    Leave me alone!

*Music. They go off. Nana comes on and sits at the side. The rest of the company come on to the dissonant and tortured chords and place themselves in contorted positions round the stage. Servants. Zoe comes on with an armload of wrapped presents.*

ZOE:    More presents for your name day, Madame.

*She remains standing and facing out during the next section.*

COOK:    *(Shouts)* Name day! Saint Nana is it?

*The other servants laugh, repeating 'Saint Nana! Saint Nana!'*

ZOE:        She says her middle name's Theresa.

MAID:       Her middle name's cunt!

BUTLER:     And her first name!

GROOM:      And her last!

            *They all laugh.*

ZOE:        Are you cooking the dinner or aren't you?

COOK:       They'll have to bloody well wait for it. We're having a
            glass of wine.

ZOE:        That's Madame's best burgundy.

BUTLER:     Have some, Zoe. Good stuff.

ZOE:        Save me a glass.

GROOM 2:    Get her to pay the feed merchant will you, Zoe?

FOOTMAN:    Ask her for it when she's got company. Then one of
            the men pays.

MAID:       It's like working in a bloody brothel here.

ZOE:        Working! You on your hands and knees scrubbing I
            suppose. The house is filthy.

MAID:       She never notices so why bother?

BUTLER:     Oh Madame Nana's not so bad. She's a good sort.

GROOM:      *(Laughs)* Because she lets you in between her legs, eh?

ZOE:        We've all seen you sneaking out of her bedroom.

COOK:       Disgusting. I'd like to spit on her backside, the slut.

GROOM:      Oooh lovely! So would I!

ZOE:        *(Sharp)* What's that you've got there?

MAID 2:     One of her gowns. She threw it away.

ZOE:        I'll take that. I get the clothes and don't you forget it.

GROOM 2:    We've polished off two cases of her champagne in the
            stables.

COOK:       Speaking of drink, let's have some more of that
            burgundy!

*Philippe comes on to Nana.*

PHILIPPE:    I've brought you a present for your name day, Nana.

NANA:        Oh you sweet boy, Philippe. *(Takes it, greedily.)* Was it
             expensive?

PHILIPPE:    Yes. *(Alarm)* Be careful of it, Nana. It's fragile.

NANA:        *(Breaking it.)* Oh the silly thing, it's broken. *(Drops it
             on the floor.)* Oh well, it was only an old antique. Don't
             cry sweetheart, if nobody ever broke anything all the
             shops would have to close down. Look at this fiddly
             thing.

             *Music. During the following section the breaking of
             the presents is done by sudden contortions of the body
             in time with the scored sounds. The movements of
             Philippe and Nana become wilder and wilder as they
             'break up' all the name day presents. The servants
             echo their movements and laugh wildly as Philippe and
             Nana smash up everything in an orgiastic frenzy.*

NANA:        And this one! Take this one, darling. *(Throws imaginary
             present to him.)* Break it! Break it! And this! And this!
             And this!

             *After the smashing up is finished music cue out. Nana
             and Philippe lie on the floor laughing and exhausted.*

NANA:        There! All gone! All smashed up! Wasn't that fun?
             Wasn't it fun!

PHILIPPE:    Yes! Fun! What a mess!

             *They kiss passionately.*

NANA:        Bring me a couple of thousand francs, precious.

PHILIPPE:    *(Aghast)* Nana . . . I can't. I can't.

NANA:        Course you can. Nana wants it. Nana needs it. *(He goes
             off. Georges comes on with a bouquet.)* Is that for me?
             *(Pulling it to bits.)* He loves me, he loves me not.
             *(Throwing flowers at him.)* He loves me, he loves me
             not . . . *(Drops flowers.)*

GEORGES:     I'll always love you, Nana. *(Goes to her.)* I saw Philippe
             going out. You're not sleeping with him. You're not
             sleeping with my brother!

*He seizes hold of her hands.*

NANA:       *(Trying to pull away.)* Oh let go of me, Georges.

            *Music.*

GEORGES:    *(Dancing her round. Singing with intensity.)* Ring a ring
            a rosies, ring a ring a rosies, ring a ring a rosies, ring
            a –

NANA:       *(During this.)* Stop it! Let me go! *(Breaks away. Music
            out.)* Yes I'm sleeping with your brother. Why
            shouldn't I?

            *She goes to sit down bad-temperedly. He takes a pair
            of scissors out of his pocket. Music. He stabs himself
            again and again to the accompaniment of chords. He
            falls. Nana screams.*

SERVANTS:   He's dead! He's killed hisself! No she killed him!
            Christ!

            *The voice of Madame Hugon is heard from offstage
            and all but the two footmen and Nana go off.*

HUGON:      My son! Where is my son? I know he's here. *(She
            comes on.)* I've come to take him – *(Sees him.)* Georges!
            *(She goes and falls on her knees beside him. Makes a
            sound of horror as she sees the wounds.)* My child!

            *Puts his head into her lap, weeping.*

GEORGES:    *(Opens his eyes)* Maman?

NANA:       *(Runs over.)* Oh thank God, he's alive! We'll put him to
            bed. I'll get the doctor.

HUGON:      Don't touch him!

NANA:       It wasn't my fault. I didn't do anything. If his brother
            were here, he'd tell you –

HUGON:      *(Hatred)* His brother is in prison. He has stolen money
            from his regiment.

GEORGES:    Maman?

HUGON:      *(Kisses him, tender.)* I'm here, darling. Maman's here.
            You'll be all right, little one. You'll be all right. I'm
            taking you home. *(To footmen.)* Come and help me

carry him, please. *(They come over and lift him and carry him off. Madame Hugon follows. Then she turns to Nana. Quietly.)* You have destroyed us, Madame.

*Music. Nana goes and picks up the scissors and begins to cut her toe nails. Muffat comes on in full chamberlain uniform. Music out.*

NANA: Muffat. What are you doing here at this time of night? And why are you all dressed up like that!

MUFFAT: I've just come from the Chamber of Deputies. Bismarck and his army are on our borders. The legislative body voted for war tonight.

NANA: How stupid.

MUFFAT: *(Sudden suspicion.)* Have you got somebody here?

NANA: None of your business.

MUFFAT: I pay for this house!

NANA: When was the last time you gave me any cash?

MUFFAT: I told you! I'm raising a loan. And I forbid you to have men in this room!

NANA: *(Dangerous, advances on him.)* What did you say? You forbid me? You? Forbid me! Listen, Chamberlain! I'll see who I want when I want and where I want. And if any man pleases me I'll go to bed with him!

MUFFAT: *(Seizing her.)* Don't say that. You don't mean it! You're mine. You belong to me!

NANA: *(Breaks away.)* I don't belong to anyone. I'm free and I do exactly what I want. *(Then giving him little punches and smiling.)* And if you don't like it, then you can go. Now. You want to go? Yes or no.

MUFFAT: No no no no no . . .

*Now the actress playing Sabine and the actor playing Fanton come swiftly forward and take the places of Nana and Muffat. She will play Nana and he will play Muffat pretending to be a dog. The actual Nana and Muffat stay at the back watching the scene and Muffat himself will speak for the dog/Muffat from the back as he watches. The rest of the company come on*

*(with the exception of the Marquis de Chouard w)*
*stands hidden behind Nana at the back) and become*
*mirror images round the stage of Nana and the*
*Muffat/dog. The Muffat/dog sinks to his knees in*
*front of Sabine/Nana.*

NANA/
SABINE:     *(Laughs)* There's a good dog. *(Pause)* Bark. Go on. *(He*
            *and the other actors playing dogs bark feebly.)* Louder!
            *(They bark much louder.)* Sit! *(He does.)* Now, beg!

            *He does. The other 'dogs' just remain crouching at the*
            *feet of the other women.*

MUFFAT:     *(From the back. Intense. Smiling a little.)* Kick me.

            *She does and the Muffat/dog howls in pain. The other*
            *actors echo this.*

NANA/
SABINE:     Do you like that?

MUFFAT:     *(From the back.)* Yes Nana. Bad doggie likes that.

            *She follows him round the stage kicking him.*

NANA/
SABINE:     And that? And that?

            *The Muffat/dog yaps and barks as do the other actors.*

MUFFAT:     *(From the back.)* Yes, Nana, yes! Hurt me.

            *The Muffat/dog sits and Sabine/Nana puts her foot*
            *hard into his groin. This action is echoed by the other*
            *women round the stage. All the 'dogs' howl.*

NANA/
SABINE:     Fetch. Go on, fetch! *(The Muffat/dog and the other*
            *actors scramble around the stage as if after a ball and take*
            *it back to the women.)* Too slow! Bad doggie! Too slow!

            *She kicks him and punches him. The other dog actors*
            *just bark and yap in chorus and the Muffat/dog.*

MUFFAT:     *(From the back.)* Hit me harder! I'm a mad dog!
            Harder!

            *The Muffat/dog growls and leaps.*

| NANA/ | |
|---|---|
| SABINE: | Now heel! *(He stops and cowers at her feet.)* Up! Up! Up! *(The Muffat/dog rises to a standing position in front of her. Then Muffat comes forward to take his place. The Muffat/dog plus the other dogs and the other women go off. Nana stands at the back still watching, Chouard half-hidden behind her.)* Now! Take this off, Chamberlain! *(He pulls off his ceremonial sash and his coat.)* Throw it on the floor! *(He does.)* Now stamp on it! Jump on it! *(He does.)* Spit on it! Go on, go on! Spit on the Chamberlain! Spit on the Chamber of Deputies! Spit on the Emperor! |

> *He does all this in a frenzy while she stands laughing at him. She goes off and Nana comes forward, Chouard holding on to her petticoats and trailing behind her. Muffat sees him. Nana is laughing.*

| MUFFAT: | *(Appalled)* Oh no! No! Not him! Oh my God! Not him! |
|---|---|
| CHOUARD: | *(Babbling)* Naughty girl made me. Poor old man. Not his fault. Dirty girl pulled all my clothes off. |
| MUFFAT: | No! Oh no! |
| CHOUARD: | *(Scuttling off.)* Poor old man. Naughty dirty girl. |
| NANA: | *(Sullen)* It's all your own fault. I needed the money. |
| MUFFAT: | Not that man! Not him! *(Flailing about in agony.)* Oh come to me, God. Help me! Let me die. Foul! Foul! Nothing but foulness . . . despair! *(Then in a kind of gabble.)* Oh my God I am heartily sorry for having offended thee. I dread the loss of heaven and the pains of hell – |
| VENOT: | *(Appearing downstage.)* Brother . . . |
| MUFFAT: | *(Throwing himself into his arms.)* Take me away! For pity's sake, take me away! |

> *Venot shepherds him off.*

| NANA: | Stupid. They're all just stupid. |
|---|---|

> *Sound of distant guns. This continues from time to time throughout the following scene. Zoe comes on.*

ZOE:            Mademoiselle Satin is in hospital, Madame. They say
                she's dying.

NANA:           Serve her right. Dirty bitch. Serve her bloody well
                right.

ZOE:            *(Going out, calm.)* And I'm giving you a week's notice,
                Madame.

NANA:           Oh Zoe, you can't! Don't! Don't go! You mustn't leave
                me!

ZOE:            Don't take on so. Madame.

NANA:           Stay!

ZOE:            *(Friendly)* Impossible, Madame. I'm sorry to leave you
                but I'm taking over La Tricon's establishment, you see.
                *(Kisses her.)* Business before feelings, Madame. You
                know that.

                        *She goes.*

NANA:           Zoe! And Satin dying . . .

LABORDETTE: *(Coming on.)* Dear girl, I've seen some quite
                magnificent lace. Exquisite! Would you like me to buy
                it for you?

NANA:           *(Eager)* Oh yes, Labordette, get it. Is there enough for
                my bed?

LABORDETTE: Yes easily, I should think. *(Casually, over his shoulder.)*
                By the way, young Hugon's died, you know.

NANA:           Zizi! Dead?

LABORDETTE: This morning.

                *Nana throws herself down on the floor sobbing.*

NANA:           Oh poor little Georges! Poor Zizi. I can't bear it, I
                can't bear it!

LABORDETTE: There there, Nana, don't cry. He was just a hysterical
                boy. It wasn't your fault.

NANA:           *(Sits up.)* No. No it wasn't, was it. I didn't ask him to
                kill himself. I didn't make him do it. But you'll see . . .
                they'll all blame me.

*During her next speech the other members of the*
*company come on and speak lines like the following.*
*(All this can be improvised by the actors.)*

1:        Not my fault.

2:        Don't look at me.

3:        I'm not responsible.

4:        Why is it always me?

5:        I'm not to blame.

6:        I didn't do anything.

*As they move they will also clear the stage and the*
*mirrored screen will be set upstage centre, folded so*
*that the mirror surface is hidden.*

NANA:     *(To Labordette.)* They'll all side against me. And I'm
          not guilty of anything. I've got a clear conscience. All
          those men. Is it my fault if they came running after
          me? They could have said no, couldn't they? They
          could have stayed away. I didn't want to hurt anybody.
          I didn't want them dropping dead all over the place. I
          didn't do anything wrong. It isn't fair!

          *Madame Lerat comes on. She is holding the doll*
          *wrapped in a black shawl.*

LERAT:    Nana! Baby's not well.

NANA:     *(Snatches the doll angrily.)* Don't be so stupid! He's
          perfectly all right. *(To doll.)* He's just been eating too
          much chocolate. *(Thrusts doll into Labordette's face.)*
          Look at his spotty little face.

LABORDETTE: *(Stares. Backs away.)* Naughty little fellow. *(Going)* I'll
          have to be getting along now, Nana. *(As he exits.)* Busy
          day.

NANA:     Do you know what I'm going to do, Auntie? I'm
          going to go away. Travel! I'm bored with Paris. You
          can take care of Louis for me. *(She hands the doll to*
          *Lerat.)* I'll sell everything. I'll go abroad. *(Music. Lerat*
          *looks down at the doll in her arms. Realises it's dead.*
          *Draws the shawl over its face and exits, Nana not noticing*
          *her go.)* I'll go all over the world and meet lots of new
          people and have a lovely lovely time. I'm going away!

*Music. Now four of the men come on and lift up the
folded screen at the back holding it up so that Nana
can walk upstage and walk under it. Then the music
becomes discordant and she strikes a series of postures
of pain and agony and falls on the floor. The men put
the screen down in front of her and open it out so that
the mirrored surface faces the audience. The four
women come on carrying chairs and sit in front of the
screen with their backs to the audience. Muffat sits
downstage facing out. Music out as they sit.
Throughout the scene the sound of gunfire, now a bit
louder.*

LUCY:          Is it true, Rose?

ROSE:          Yes. She's dying.

               *Fauchery comes on from upstage and goes down to the
               front. Calls across to another actor opposite.*

FAUCHERY:      Mignon. I heard Nana was here at the Grand Hotel.

MIGNON:        *(Calls back.)* Yes. My wife brought her here, God
               knows why. Fauchery, go up there and tell Rose to
               come out of that room.

FAUCHERY:      Go yourself.

MUFFAT:        *(Stands)* Is the person upstairs any better?

VOICE:         *(Off)* No change, Monsieur.

TATAN:         How is she?

ROSE:          Sinking fast. *(Shudders)* You wouldn't recognise her.

BLANCHE:       Poor girl. Oh poor girl.

TATAN:         Remember her as Venus? Where would you find
               another body like that. Those shoulders! Those legs!
               What breasts!

ROSE:          *(Shudders again violently.)* She's changed. Oh God!
               She's changed.

               *During the last couple of speeches there is the sound of
               crowds shouting in the streets outside the hotel and
               louder gunfire. Fanton comes on. Goes to Mignon.*

| | |
|---|---|
| FANTON: | She's here? I'll go up and see her. *(Starts to go.)* What's wrong with her? |
| MIGNON/ FAUCHERY: | Smallpox. |
| FANTON: | *(Horror)* Smallpox? *(Stops)* Jesus! |
| VOICES: | *(With some of company on stage joining in.)* To Berlin! To Berlin! |
| BORDENAVE: | *(Coming on.)* Bloody crowds. I could hardly get through. How is she? |
| VOICES: | *(As before.)* To Berlin! To Berlin! |
| FAUCHERY: | Fools. March on Berlin? Bismarck's about to invade Paris. |
| FANTON: | We'll fight for the Emperor! |
| FAUCHERY: | You're joking. The Emperor's finished. |
| LUCY: | Listen to the crowd. |
| VOICES: | To Berlin! To Berlin! |
| TATAN: | *(Shivers)* War. |
| BLANCHE: | What's going to become of us? |
| LUCY: | I've just bought a house in Passy. It'll be burned to the ground if there's an invasion. |
| BORDENAVE: | *(Nod to Muffat.)* Is that. . . ? |
| MIGNON: | Count Muffat. Been here all night. |
| BLANCHE: | I'll go to London. I'm not staying here to be killed. |
| TATAN: | There'll be plenty of military men about. |
| LUCY: | Prussians. |
| TATAN: | So? |
| FANTON: | Those women are mad to be up there with her. |
| MIGNON: | Why doesn't Rose come down? She'll look bloody marvellous if she catches it. Holes all over her face. |
| LUCY: | Has she suffered much? |

ROSE:    *(With revulsion.)* Hideously. Her face – her whole body . . . bloated, rotten, covered in sores. Oh God! She's just a heap of pus and blood.

BLANCHE:    Horrible! Oh how horrible.

ROSE:    *(Dully)* Yes. It's funny isn't it. We always hated each other but this has been such a blow to me. Sitting here with her I've been having all kinds of strange ideas. Wanting to die myself . . . feeling that the end of the world is coming . . .

LUCY:    What's that noise?

    *Sound of a fly buzzing. It gets louder and louder. Stops. Silence.*

MUFFAT:    Is the person upstairs . . .

ALL:    Dead.

VOICES:    *(All the actors joining in this time.)* To Berlin! To Berlin!

    *They go on shouting this as they carry the chairs off as at the beginning of the play. Then they all (including Nana) take positions upstage in couples for the Mazurka. They dance downstage, their faces stern. They break and the men walk upstage and off to return doing a slow march across the stage as if they are soldiers going to war. The women stand in various places on the stage watching them expressionlessly. Then they make their way off going through and around the line of men. The last woman off looks after the men as they go off. Then she goes off. The lights fade to blackout and the music fades with the lights.*

### THE END

# GERMINAL

94

# INTRODUCTION

Dramatising a novel for the stage is an entirely pointless task if it is merely an end in itself. Despite being a good starting-point, enthusiasm for the original text is not on its own a sufficient reason. After all, loyalties to both the original author *and* a theatre-going audience have to be respected and there are occasions when they appear to be in contradiction. The finishing-point then must be to produce a play that exists in its own right, and if a certain amount of ransacking and rearranging is needed to do this . . . then so be it.

As far as the particular demands of GERMINAL are concerned then, no apologies to Zola for the inventions (in particular M. Hennebeau's drunken denunciation of his wife's infidelity), or the omissions (Cecile's strangulation), not to mention the fifty or sixty characters that never made it from page to stage. Liberties have likewise been taken with the dialogue, of which understandably there is very little in the novel. An integral part of the dramatisation, as in the writing of any play, was to find the 'voice' of the various characters involved, not only as individuals with particular personalities, but as members of a class and above all a close-knit community. Short of requiring the actors to speak in fake French accents, a hazardous option, the best idea seemed to be to choose an equivalent British dialect that would express by implication not only the nature of the work but also the communal identity of the workers, as opposed to anything geographical. The Yorkshire dialect I think achieves this, particularly in contrast with the formality of the Bourgeois speech, while allowing the likes of M. Deneulin, the self-made man, to fall uneasily between the two. Chaval in the original is an 'ousider', hence the Scottish, whereas Etienne's language is sufficiently neutral to allow him to come from anywhere so long as it is outside the community. The retention of French denominations in spite of this is simply in order to reaffirm where the action physically takes place.

Perhaps the most controversial decision concerned the ending; in the novel Etienne survives his ordeal underground, emerges 'a wiser man', and moves on from Montsou, both in order to satisfy the conventions of Naturalism (later to form the basis of innumerable cowboy films) and in order to star in the next Zola novel. What seemed important to me was for an audience to leave the theatre with the same sense of elation that is contained in the final chapter of the novel, rather than any concern as to whether or not Etienne the individual lives or dies. In this respect the final scene with Etienne and Catherine making love in the belly of the earth, a well-prepared image that carries Zola's sense of belief in a New Era, seemed most appropriate.

So much for the surgery; as with historical drama, it is the overall ideas that need to be protected and remain constant, rather than the individual components, and in this context Zola's GERMINAL had a very particular appeal. Certainly it is a passionate, epic drama with a strong 'domestic' story-line and a cast of characters positively itching to make an entrance, indeed, much of its construction has an innate theatricality. But it is the contemporary flavour of its ideas that fascinate. Written in the late nineteenth century, it was the first novel of its generation to examine the struggle between Capital and Labour and managed to do so without stereotyping either its villains or its heroes: what emerges is not Liberalism; Zola makes it perfectly clear who has the easier time, but the recognition that ultimately under this system *no one* can lead a happy and fulfilled life.

For anyone who doubts the relevance of the piece, you need only look back at the decade that has just passed; ten years that included a year-long Miners' Strike (with fatalities), inner City riots, the murder of P.C. Blakelock, three million unemployed, and at least two Royal Weddings . . . in fact it is not hard to find a modern equivalent for almost every major event in the play. The time and place may have shifted, but the cause and effect most certainly haven't. Above all, the nineties have been ushered in with the most extraordinary displays of 'people power' that we have seen for many years. While the Right misguidedly choose to dance with undisguised pleasure on the 'grave of Socialism' (for the most part in hobnail boots), the Left are busy regrouping themselves in an attempt to redefine what Socialism actually is. In this period of self-examination, we must grasp what few certainties are on offer. GERMINAL if nothing else is about the celebration of resistance and the belief in a more equitable future. We could do worse than to take heart from this optimism in the knowledge that if present battles are lost, it is for future wars to be won. What better reason for bringing it to the stage?

I should finally thank Paines Plough The Writers' Company and Pip Broughton for their persistence and courage in putting on an epic play at a time when Government Arts policy is entirely hostile to any new play-writing that involves more than four characters and whose political content exceeds that of a marsh-mallow.

WILLIAM GAMINARA
May 1990

GERMINAL received its British première in this dramatisation in a co-production between Paines Plough the Writers' Company, Plymouth Theatre Royal and Derby Playhouse at The Drum, Plymouth Theatre Royal in September 1988. The cast was as follows:

| | |
|---|---|
| CHAVAL | Stewart Porter |
| DENEULIN | Owen John O'Mahony |
| ETIENNE | Robert Patterson |
| M. GREGOIRE | Godfrey Jackman |
| CECILE GREGOIRE | Catherine Cusack |
| M. HENNEBEAU | Robin Soans |
| MME HENNEBEAU | Lois Baxter |
| LEVAQUE | James Bryce |
| MME LEVAQUE | Eileen Pollock |
| CATHERINE LEVAQUE | Debra Gillett |
| MAIGRAT | Edward York |
| NEGREL | Christopher Kent |
| RASSENEUR | Ian Blower |
| SOUVARINE | Stafford Gordon |

| | |
|---|---|
| DIRECTOR | Pip Broughton |
| DESIGNER | Simon Vincenzi |
| LIGHTING DESIGNER | Jim Simmons |
| MUSICAL DIRECTOR | Andy Dodge |

The single stroke "/" in the middle of a speech indicates the point at which the following character should begin speaking.

# ACT ONE

## SCENE ONE

*Pitch darkness. The sound of a violent storm can be heard, particularly a high gale blowing in the distance. We are indoors so it should not be full volume. Suddenly a candle is lit, which after a second moves urgently across the stage, carried by Monsieur Levaque though he is virtually unseen to us. It is placed beside a figure lying asleep on the floor. It is Catherine. He shakes her.*

LEVAQUE: *(In a whisper.)* Catherine . . . Catherine! . . . Grandad's home . . . *(There is no response.)* . . . Catherine! . . . *(He shakes her again. She wakes with a start and then sinks back as if unwilling to be awake.)* . . . come on, it's after four . . . buckle to . . .

> *Leaving the candle he moves off stage. From the other side an older figure arrives in the darkness. He stands silently by Catherine as she gets up. The moment she leaves her sleeping place, he climbs in. Not a word is exchanged. She picks up the candle and walks off stage. As she moves off, Monsieur Gregoire tiptoes on from the other side wearing his dressing-gown and holding a night-light. He tiptoes over to another sleeping figure and holds the light to it, lighting up the cherubic face of Cecile in a deep sleep. He leans over.*

GREGOIRE: *(Whispering)* Cecile . . .

> *There is no response. He smiles, leans over and kisses her gently on the cheek, before tip-toeing off again. As he moves off, light comes up on the half-dressed figure of Monsieur Hennebeau. He is sitting on the bed of Madame Hennebeau who lies fast asleep. Slowly he runs his hand over the full shape of her body. He leans over.*

HENNEBEAU: *(Whispering)* Helene . . . Helene! . . .

> *There is no response. He runs his hand over her again. This time the figure rolls over, away from him. Resigned, he stands and continues dressing. The lights fade on him. Once again we are in total darkness.*

*Now the sound of the wind and rain becomes louder as
we move out of doors to the pit-head, backed by the
sound of machinery. The following scene thus all takes
place in a form of dumb show. A gleam of light
appears on the horizon and we see small clusters of
miners, in twos and threes, waiting to go down. If
possible, from time to time, several miners disappear
into a mouthlike cage that takes them to the coalface.
New arrivals replace them giving the impression of an
endless conveyor belt bringing on miners and feeding
them to the pit. All the while the light gradually grows
and the wind rages. The miners talk to each other as
they await their turn though we cannot hear what
they say. Monsieur Hennebeau walks purposefully
across the back of the stage and momentarily
conversation stops as they watch him. Once gone, they
resume their talk. It is at this point that Etienne
Lantier arrives, a cold, drenched figure carrying a
small bundle. He sees the waiting miners, thinks about
speaking to them but decides to pass them by. Just as
he is about to exit, a loud siren blares out above the
noise of the wind and liftshaft, stopping him in his
tracks. Seeing men disappear into the cage, he decides
to approach them after all and turns back. The miners
pay him little attention as he wanders amongst them
asking for work. All shake their head and point him in
different directions, including a group of miners made
up of Levaque, Chaval and Catherine who have just
arrived. Having asked everyone, he is just about to set
off again when, following urgent conversation between
Catherine and her father, much to Chaval's
disapproval Catherine runs off and fetches Etienne
back. It seems there is work for him after all. Visibly
delighted we see him shaking hands vigorously with his
new workmates before another blast on the siren calls
them off to the cage. As we move from this prologue to
the first scene the sound of the wind gradually fades as
the sound of the machinery (different from the faint
machinery we heard above ground) gradually grows to
a deafening pitch. We are now five hundred metres
underground, Levaque and Chaval are digging. They
have stripped off to the waist. The general impression
should be one of immensely cramped surroundings and*

*unbearable heat in contrast to the cold up above.*
*Etienne and Catherine are apart from the other two.*
*Levaque and Chaval start shouting at one another and*
*pointing at parts of the tunnel. It is clear they are*
*arguing though we can not hear what they are saying.*
*The noise of the machinery stops, exposing their*
*conversation.*

LEVAQUE:  *(Shouting)* Have done, will tha . . . these mines have
ears.

*Cheers can be heard all round.*

CHAVAL:  Then I hope they're listenin' oot . . . it's mair than
Monsieur Hennebeau'll ever dae.

LEVAQUE:  Hush up, I say . . . if it's trouble you're aimin' at, wait
till you're on your own.

CHAVAL:  . . . ah weel, he's problems o' his ain tae be shair.

LEVAQUE:  Aye. When tha's all clogged up wit' honey, tha can't
allus rise and fly, so they say.

CHAVAL:  Ay, but they're ay the yin tae say it.

*Etienne has stopped working and is watching them.*

CATHERINE:  Take no 'count on them . . . they're allus yellin' i' that
road.

ETIENNE:  You don't.

CATHERINE:  I've no call to.

LEVAQUE:  *(Seeing them chat.)* Hoy! . . . buckle to or there'll be
trouble.

CATHERINE:  But pump's stopped.

LEVAQUE:  And what by that? *(To Chaval.)* She's half asleep.

CHEVAL:  I doot there'll be many as slept wi' a' that wind n' rain
the nicht. I thoucht the end o' the world were nigh.
*(To Etienne and Catherine.)* We're up ower oor knees in
coal heer . . . we cannae dig AND load. *(Catherine
moves over to collect the coal.)* . . . calls hi'self a flamin'
haulier. . . . I've seen mair brawn on a week-auld bairn.

LEVAQUE:  He'll sharpen up through time.

CATHERINE: They're not takin' coal no more, not wit' pump
stopped.

LEVAQUE: What! *(Beat)* Why now then, let's have summat to eat.

> *They stop where they are and remove their-butties from
> under their jackets.*

CATHERINE: Are you not eatin'?

ETIENNE: No . . . no, I'm not hungry.

CATHERINE: Not hungry! You must be . . . have some o' mine.

ETIENNE: No, no really.

CATHERINE: Why, if you don't like the look of it.

ETIENNE: Oh no, it's not that, it's just . . . *(She offers it to him.
He hesitates and then takes it. They eat ravenously.)* Is it
nearly time to stop?

> *Catherine laughs and then realises it's a serious
> question.*

CATHERINE: It's nobbut summat after eight! *(Pause.)* Water?

ETIENNE: No thanks.

CATHERINE: You'll most likely choke if you swallow it dry.

ETIENNE: No really, I'm alright.

CATHERINE: If I drink first, will tha take some after?

> *She takes a swig and passes it to him.*

ETIENNE: Thanks.

> *He takes a swig. Meantime Chaval has come over.*

CHAVAL: And hoo are the lassies doin' in this wee corner?

CATHERINE: Goin' on nicely thank you.

CHAVAL: I hope I'm no' interruptin' onythin'. . . . You twa seem
tae to be gettin' on like a hoose on fire.

CATHERINE: Go away . . .

CHAVAL: Tch tch . . . and I only came ower tae gi'e ye an

apple . . . *(Etienne and Catherine watch the apple.)* . . .
you're no' tellin' me you dinnae want it? *(She puts her
hand out to take it.)* . . . uh uh uh . . . no graspin' and
grabbin', where are your manners. . . ? *(She takes her
hand back.)* . . . still, to show ye that I've no ill-feelin'
aboot it . . .

> *He leans over, hands her the apple and kisses her full on the
> lips. She pushes him off.*

CATHERINE: Oh get off! *(He laughs and moves off. Catherine wipes
her lips and notices Etienne staring at her.)* . . . what's
wit' thee?

ETIENNE: I thought . . .

CATHERINE: I reckon nowt o' him if that's what you're thinkin' . . .
he nobbut fools about nows and thens . . .

ETIENNE: No . . . it's just that . . . I thought you were a boy.

CATHERINE: Me? A lad? Look. *(She takes her hat off to reveal her
hair all piled up. They laugh. He continues staring at
her.)* . . . have you not seen a lass before?

NEGREL: *(Off)* Yes . . . yes, alright. I've found it now.

LEVAQUE: Nay damn, what did I tell thee . . . they rise up out o'
the ground. Come on stir yourselves . . . *(They begin
work again in silence. Paul Negrel appears.)* Good day to
you Monsieur Negrel . . .

NEGREL: Good day Levaque. I understand we took on a new
man this morning.

LEVAQUE: Aye Monsieur . . . *(Calls)* Etienne . . .

CHAVAL: There should be twa women in each team . . .

LEVAQUE: I've a notion we'll get a sight more work done wit' one.

> *Negrel holds up a lamp up to inspect Etienne.*

NEGREL: What's your name?

ETIENNE: Etienne Lantier.

NEGREL: How old are you?

ETIENNE:    Twenty.

NEGREL:     Have you been down a mine before?

ETIENNE:    As an engineer, yes. *(Beat)* . . . apprentice . . .

NEGREL:     Alright. *(To Levaque.)* But I don't much like the idea of
            taking on an unknown man off the road. It's hard work
            down here . . . for all of us . . . and not just anybody
            can do it.

LEVAQUE:    I nobbut thought . . .

NEGREL:     I know what you thought and between you and me I
            agree. But you know what they're like up above. So
            don't make a habit of it. At least not without consulting
            me first, there's a good fellow. *(To Etienne.)* Where are
            you staying?

ETIENNE:    Uh . . .

LEVAQUE:    With Monsieur Rasseneur . . . *(Negrel looks sharply at
            Levaque.)* . . . till he finds some place else.

NEGREL:     Let's hope it doesn't take too long, for your sake.
            Alright, let's get back to work, shall we . . . *(They
            continue working as Negrel looks around the tunnel.)*
            Good God Levaque, don't you give a damn for
            anybody. Look at this timbering man . . . you'll end up
            being buried alive down here.

LEVAQUE:    It's sturdy enough Monsieur, no word of a lie . . .

NEGREL:     Sturdy!

CHAVAL:     We've had nae problems no far.

NEGREL:     So far, yes. Are you really telling me you'd prefer to
            have your skulls caved in than to leave the cutting and
            spend a little more time on the timbering? I'm sorry,
            I've no alternative but to fine your team three francs
            . . . and it's no good you shaking your head at me
            Chaval, these are Company regulations not mine. If
            you continue like this, they'll quite simply alter the rate
            of payment. In the meanwhile retimber all that
            immediately. *(Pause)* I'll be round again tomorrow. I
            hope I've made myself clear.

LEVAQUE:    Aye Monsieur.

*He starts to leave but is unsure of the way.*

NEGREL:     Now . . . how do I get out of here. . . ?

CHAVAL:     Doonwards . . .

LEVAQUE:    Yon road'll take you out Monsieur . . .

            *He leaves.*

CHEVAL:     Hell and Damnation! They're ay a'greetin' for
            somethin'!

LEVAQUE:    Nay damn, I'll not stand for 'owt o' that back-talk.
            Givin' him thy lip'll not help us 'owt!

CHAVAL:     And keepin' your mouth shut will? He's lucky my lip's
            a' I did gi'e him . . .

LEVAQUE:    It doesn't do to lay thy own offences at someone else's
            door. *(Pause)* At all events, it's to no use us mafflin' on
            in this gate. . . . Catherine, get shot o' that corf and set
            to wit' timberin'. Etienne you'll have to. . . . *(Etienne is
            still gazing after Negrel.)* . . . Etienne!

ETIENNE:    Sorry, yes?

LEVAQUE:    You'll have to manage on your own for now. *(The
            machinery starts up again. Jeers can be heard in the
            distance. . . . Levaque shouts:)* . . . Welcome to
            Montsou!

            *They continue work.*

# SCENE TWO

*The lights fade on the labouring men and rise simultaneously on the
Gregoire household, where Monsieur Gregoire sits with the newspaper at
the breakfast table. There should be a second or two when both are
visible. During this slow exchange of lighting areas, quite separately we
see Madame Levaque, clutching a baby, walking across stage in the
direction of the Gregoires. Out of the fading noise of machinery from the
previous scene, there is the sound of a grandfather clock striking the hour.
Once the change-over is complete and Madame Levaque has disappeared,
we stay with Monsieur Gregoire. It is very light and warm. He looks up
at the ceiling, chuckles to himself, and continues reading. The door bursts
open and Cecile comes in.*

| M. | |
|---|---|
| GREGOIRE: | Ah . . . bravo . . . the sleeping beauty awakes . . . |
| CECILE: | Papa! Breakfast without me . . . how could you! |
| M. GREGOIRE: | Don't worry my darling, I waited especially for you. Welcome to the land of the living. *(They embrace.)* . . . I thought that the storm must have kept you awake last night so I gave the strictest instructions to Cook not to start until you were down. |
| CECILE: | Was there a storm? I had no idea. Oh what dreams I've had Papa, what dreams . . . |
| M. GREGOIRE: | Pleasant ones, I trust . . . Now sit yourself down . . . |

*Cook enters carrying some hot coffee and a brioche.*

| COOK: | Good mornin' to you Mademoiselle . . . |
|---|---|
| CECILE: | Ooh brioche! Is this especially for me? |
| M. GREGOIRE: | Who else? |
| CECILE: | Oh thank you Papa . . . |

*She kisses him again.*

| M. GREGOIRE: | Cook's the person you really have to thank . . . she made it with her own fair hands. |
|---|---|
| CECILE: | You're so clever cook. . . . I wouldn't know where to begin . . . |
| M. GREGOIRE: | Well you'll have to learn before too long my dear, that's for sure . . . |
| CECILE: | Papa . . . |
| COOK: | Now don't you go embarrassin' the young lass, Monsieur Gregoire . . . see now, she's all coloured up . . . all in good time. |
| CECILE: | Thank you cook. Isn't he wicked. |

*There is a knock at the front foor.*

| | |
|---|---|
| M. GREGOIRE: | Who in Heaven's name can that be? |
| COOK: | Are you at home Monsieur? |
| M. GREGOIRE: | *(Reluctant)* Yes . . . yes, I am. |
| CECILE: | Oh if it's the tutor, tell him I'm ill today . . . |
| M. GREGOIRE: | Now, now Cecile, we'll have none of that . . . it's not as if you have to have lessons all day and every day, is it . . . |
| CECILE: | I don't see why I should have lessons at all any more . . . |
| M. GREGOIRE: | Oh don't you . . . you'd be happier eating brioche all day I suppose . . . |
| COOK: | Monsieur Deneulin to see you, Monsieur. |
| M. GREGOIRE: | What a pleasant surprise. Show him in. *(Monsieur Deneulin enters.)* . . . Good Morning Pierre, come on in. |
| M. DENEULIN: | Good Mornin' to you Leon . . . Cecile . . . Oh I'm sorry, am I interruptin'? |
| M. GREGOIRE: | Oh no, not to worry. To be quite honest, we are a little late this morning. |
| CECILE: | Won't you join us Monsieur Deneulin? |
| M. DENEULIN: | Thank you kindly, but I'll not be stayin' long; although I must say it does look good. |
| CECILE: | Oh go on . . . |
| M. DENEULIN: | No, no. . . . I've already eaten thank you very much. But please, don't mind me. |

M.
GREGOIRE:    Another coffee cup please Cook . . . so. To what do we
             owe the pleasure of your company Pierre?

M.
DENEULIN:    Oh nothin' special really. I were just out for a ride to
             loosen up the joints you know, and passin' by I thought
             I'd look in to see how you were both keepin'.

M.
GREGOIRE:    That's very thoughtful of you. How's the family?

M.
DENEULIN:    Goin' on nicely thank you. Very nicely. Lucie sings
             from dawn through till dusk . . . and Marie-Anne I
             fear . . . has taken to paintin' . . .

CECILE:      Painting!

M.
DENEULIN:    Aye. *(Cecile exchanges looks with her father.)* . . . I'm
             sure it's only a passin' thing . . . and why not . . .
             *(Beat)*

M.
GREGOIRE:    And what about Vandame . . . how are things there, I
             don't see a new carriage outside . . .

M.
DENEULIN:    . . . a new carriage outside . . . no, no, this blasted
             crisis is not helpin' me one little bit Leon.

M.
GREGOIRE:    I don't imagine it's helping anyone.

M.
DENEULIN:    Things aren't desperate mind, but . . . thus far it's
             been so easy. If you'd sold up like I said and invested
             your money in our mine at Vandame, you'd be a rich
             man today.

M.
GREGOIRE:    But I am a rich man Pierre. And I am rich precisely
             because I will not speculate.

M.
DENEULIN:    . . . not speculate . . . I'm not talkin' about speculation.
             I'm talkin' about investment and they're as far from
             one another as chalk and cheese.

M.
GREGOIRE:    Really Pierre . . .

CECILE:      Sugar Monsieur Deneulin?

M.
DENEULIN:    Please, two.

M.
GREGOIRE:    I'm surprised at you . . . when my great
             Grandfather . . .

CECILE:      Oh Papa do we have to . . .

M.
GREGOIRE:    . . . yes we do . . . when my . . .

CECILE:      We're having breakfast . . .

M.
GREGOIRE:    . . . when my great Grandfather bought this property,
             he didn't buy it because he thought that one day he
             could sell it and make a vast amount of money to buy
             this and to do that . . . he bought it for his family to
             live in and for his family's family to live in and so on,
             for as long as there were Gregoires to live here . . .

M.
DENEULIN:    But I'm not talkin' about . . .

M.
GREGOIRE:    . . . and thanks be to God otherwise we wouldn't be
             sitting here now eating brioche and drinking coffee. *(To
             Cecile who is offering him more coffee.)* . . . please, yes
             . . . *(To Deneulin.)* . . . of course I could sell my . . .
             *(To Cecile.)* . . . thank you that's enough . . . *(To
             Deneulin.)* Yes, I could sell my stake in the
             Company. . . . I could pour all the proceeds into some
             cock-eyed enterprise . . .

M.
DENEULIN:    Vandame is no cock-eyed enterprise!

M.
GREGOIRE:    Forgive me Pierre, I'm not saying it is . . . what I am
             saying is that there is something called faith, a little of
             which would do you no harm. The fact is that money
             makes money, and as long as it continues . . . to do so I
             . . .

M.
DENEULIN:        What if Montsou goes bankrupt . . . there's bound to
                 be a deep decline . . . in the. . . ?

M.
GREGOIRE:        Faith Pierre, have a little faith. So we're going through
                 a difficult period, that's unfortunate but things will get
                 better again, for everyone . . . including Cecile's
                 children . . .

                     *Pause.*

M.
DENEULIN:        So . . . if I perhaps were to talk about you maybe
                 puttin' a thousand francs into Vandame, you'd not be
                 . . . *(Monsieur Gregoire looks suitably shocked.)* . . . I'm
                 only speculatin' mind . . . I weren't. . . . By Heavens,
                 we're not as hard set as all that . . .

M.
GREGOIRE:        Oh yes you are. The truth of the matter is that you're a
                 very little fish in a very big pond; if I were you, I
                 should sell fast before the big fish come and gobble you
                 up.

M.
DENEULIN:        Never. As long as I breathe Montsou'll not have
                 Vandame. I met with Monsieur Hennebeau Thursday
                 last . . . and do you know, even he is beginnin' to crawl
                 all over me just like that crowd from Paris crawled all
                 over me when they came down last Autumn . . .

M.
GREGOIRE:        Would you rather they walked all over you?

M.
DENEULIN:        I'd rather they left me alone altogether. If they'd half
                 the chance they'd have the shirt from off my back. I'm
                 damned if I'm goin' to give them the satisfaction of
                 sellin' just so as they can rule the roost. Never! Not
                 while I'm of this world. Never!

                     *There is a knock at the main door.*

CECILE:          That must be the tutor Papa . . . goodbye Monsieur
                 Deneulin.

M.
DENEULIN:        Goodbye Cecile . . .

CECILE: Don't let Papa upset you too much . . .

M.
DENEULIN: No, no . . . don't you concern yourself. I'm made of sterner stuff than that.

M.
GREGOIRE: And don't you forget you're going shopping with Madame Hennebeau later on . . .

CECILE: I won't.

*She exits. Pause. Monsieur Gregoire helps himself to brioche.*

M.
DENEULIN: How are things progressin' with young Paul Negrel?

M.
GREGOIRE: Nothing is settled yet. . . ; it's still early days but sometimes I think I can hear wedding bells in the not so distant distance.

M.
DENEULIN: Well I hope they settle it all out.

M.
GREGOIRE: You don't approve of the idea.

M.
DENEULIN: Oh Leon, I wish them all the best naturally. Monsieur Hennebeau and I have our differences I own . . . but she's not keepin' company with him is she . . .

M.
GREGOIRE: And Paul?

M.
DENEULIN: A nice enough young man . . . hard workin', a sense of humour. . . . I'm sure they'll make a worthy couple. *(Pause)* Of course . . . it has been whispered that he and his aunt have been . . .

M.
GREGOIRE: Pierre, I forbid you to continue . . .

M.
DENEULIN: I'm only sayin' what I've . . .

M.
GREGOIRE:    Pierre!

             *Cecile enters.*

CECILE:      It wasn't the tutor Papa, it's that woman we met.

M.
GREGOIRE:    Who?

CECILE:      The miner's wife . . . Madame Levaque . . .

M.
GREGOIRE:    Oh . . .

CECILE:      You did say that she should come round.

M.
GREGOIRE:    I know.

CECILE:      . . . and she does look miserable Papa. Perhaps we
             should give her a franc or two . . .

M.
GREGOIRE:    Now, now, now Cecile . . . this is God's house and
             God demands that we be charitable; you know very
             well that I should be only too happy to make some
             donation if I thought it would be spent on common
             necessaries and not instead in the public-house, where
             one indiscretion simply leads to another; charity in kind
             Cecile if you don't mind . . . give her the clothes from
             upstairs. *(Pause)* And let's see that smile back on your
             face . . . that's better, that's the face I like best.

             *Just as Cecile is about to leave, as an act of defiance,
             she deliberately walks over to the breakfast table, picks
             up the remains of the brioche and leaves.*

M.
DENEULIN:    *(Laughing)* She's too kind for her own good that girl.

M.
GREGOIRE:    Pierre, I won't pretend that it is the first time that I
             have heard that disgraceful rumour. But I assure you
             that it is exactly that . . . a disgraceful rumour.
             Madame Hennebeau is a lady of great distinction.
             Moreover she is some fourteen years older than her
             nephew.

M.
DENEULIN:  I'm sure you're right.

M.
GREGOIRE:  Besides it was she herself who suggested that Paul and
           Cecile might take an interest in each other in the very
           first instance. So we'll hear no more on that subject if
           you don't mind.

M.
DENEULIN:  You have my word. As you say it's doubtless no more
           than an ugly rumour. Any road, enough of this rampin'
           and ravin', I must be leavin' you; there's a deal of work
           to be done.

M.
GREGOIRE:  Well don't forget to come back and visit us again soon.
           We'll set you a place at the breakfast table next time.

M.
DENEULIN:  I shall look forward to it. And think on what I said
           Leon . . . don't forget . . .

M.
GREGOIRE:  How could I Pierre, how could I . . .

M.
DENEULIN:  Oh don't bother with seein' me out. I know my own
           way by now.

M.
GREGOIRE:  Farewell.

           *He exits. Monsieur Gregoire returns to his breakfast
           but seems to have lost his appetite for the piece of
           brioche that now lies, all buttered, in front of him.*

# SCENE THREE

*Monsieur Gregoire remains seated and still visible for a few seconds as we
hear Madame Hennebeau approaching from off stage. As she enters,
followed by Cecile laden with shopping bags, lights fade on the Gregoire
household. It is almost as if we have moved to the character he is thinking
about. The two women walk towards Maigrat's shop.*

MME
HENNEBEAU: What I utterly fail to understand is how anyone can
actually like the country . . . endless fields, endless hills
. . . tiny, insignificant streets leading to tiny
insignificant places, filled with equally insignificant
people. *(They reach Maigrat's.)* . . . talking of which, I
do believe the end is in sight Cecile, this is positively
our last port of call. Now . . . promise me you won't
allow me to drag you off anywhere else afterwards.

CECILE:     I promise . . .

MME
HENNEBEAU: Good girl. *(They enter the shop.)* . . . good afternoon
Monsieur Maigrat . . .

MAIGRAT:    Madame Hennebeau, what an agreeable surprise. And
Mademoiselle Cecile, how nice to see you both. May I
say how pretty we're looking today Mademoiselle . . .

CECILE:     Why thank you.

MME
HENNEBEAU: You certainly may not or I shall feel neglected.

MAIGRAT:    Madame, for you it goes without saying. And how is
Monsieur?

MME
HENNEBEAU: Oh the same as ever, you know. In Paris today as it
happens, wining and dining with the powers that
be . . .

MAIGRAT:    Where Madame would also dearly like to be . . .

MME
HENNEBEAU: In Paris, yes . . . wining and dining, yes . . . but in that
company, very definitely no.

CECILE:     How is the business Monsieur Maigrat?

MAIGRAT:    Tidy enough, Mademoiselle, thank you very much; but
then I have such a generous landlord, even if he will
swan off to Paris from time to time . . .

MME
HENNEBEAU: *(Produces a list from her bag and hands it to Maigrat.)*
Here we are . . .

MAIGRAT: . . . not to mention my landlord's good wife who is the best customer to be had in Montsou . . .

MME
HENNEBEAU: Flattery will get you everywhere Monsieur Maigrat. I hope you have everything.

MAIGRAT: Oh I should say so. Will we be settling this at the end of the month Madame or . . .

MME
HENNEBEAU: No. no . . . I'll pay for it directly . . .

MAIGRAT: Very well. *(He moves around collecting the various items. Cecile wanders around the shop.)* . . . let's have a look now . . . something of a party I see; while the cat's away, why not?

MME
HENNEBEAU: Why not indeed Monsieur. These are such dreary days.

MAIGRAT: Well I'm afraid they're getting longer Madame . . . though you'd not think it . . . there's scarcely a bud on the trees. . . . At all events I hear that before long you'll have good cause to celebrate . . . or perchance Mademoiselle is better disposed to answer that.

CECILE: Monsieur?

MAIGRAT: I were just saying Mademoiselle . . . *(Madame Hennebeau silences him.)* I were just wondering if there was perhaps anything I might get for you . . .

CECILE: No thank you very much. I've really only come to restrain Madame . . .

MAIGRAT: Then I'm afraid you've not done very well.

CECILE: Oh dear.

MAIGRAT: Don't you listen to the young lady, Madame, you enjoy yourself while you can, that's what I say. Now then, let's just write all this down. *(He makes a note of the items. Quietly.)* Yes, I expect you'll miss the young man, won't you . . .

MME
HENNEBEAU: Yes . . . yes, I expect I will. *(Pause. Madame Levaque, wearing a red shawl, appears, walking towards Maigrat's.)* Let's struggle back then, Cecile, before I think of

something else. Farewell Monsieur Maigrat and thank you . . .

MAIGRAT:    Not at all Madame, it's always a pleasure. Goodbye Mademoiselle. I look forward to seeing you both again.

> *They exit, Madame Hennebeau talking all the while. As they leave, Madame Levaque sees them. She stops and quickly removes the red shawl, placing it with the bundle of clothes given to her by Cecile in the previous scene. She continues walking. As they cross, Madame Levaque acknowledges Cecile, indicating thanks for the bundle of clothes. This all happens over the following dialogue.*

MME
HENNEBEAU: I'm surprised Maigrat's is still standing after last night. I was convinced the roof was going to blow off the house. Marcel needless to say positively adores thunder and lightning. As far as I can make out he spent most of last night with his nose glued to the window-pane, no doubt willing it to happen. It's April for Goodness sake . . . . anyone would think we were being punished. . . .

MME
LEVAQUE:    Mademoiselle . . .

> *Cecile smiles and walks off with Madame Hennebeau. Madame Levaque stops outside Maigrat's as if deciding whether to go in or not. Just as she makes the decision not to enter, she hears Cecile calling.*

CECILE:     Madame Levaque. . . !

> *Cecile runs back on and presses a franc piece into Madame Levaque's hand before running straight off again.*

MME
LEVAQUE:    Oh thank you Mademoiselle, thank you . . . and God bless you . . . *(She turns, puts on the shawl again, and enters Maigrat's.)* . . . good afternoon Monsieur Maigrat, I'm afraid it's me again.

MAIGRAT:    Good afternoon Madame . . .

| | |
|---|---|
| MME LEVAQUE: | How's Madame Maigrat? |
| MAIGRAT: | She's still poorly, I'm afraid. But she'll be glad to hear you asked after her. |
| MME LEVAQUE: | I'm sorry about last week . . . |
| MAIGRAT: | Oh not to worry . . . |
| MME LEVAQUE: | . . . but Grandad were as lame . . . as a three legged dog and . . . |
| MAIGRAT: | There's no need to fetch all that up. We'll let bygones be bygones shall we. Now what can I do for you today? |
| MME LEVAQUE: | I were wonderin' if you had a couple o' loaves left and some coffee and . . . let me think . . . |
| MAIGRAT: | You are able to pay this time Madame. . . ? |
| MME LEVAQUE: | Oh aye Monsieur . . . |

*She holds up her franc.*

| | |
|---|---|
| MAIGRAT: | Forgive me for asking but you do understand, I too have a rent to pay and there is still that small matter of twenty francs to be straightened up. You haven't forgotten that now, have you Madame? |
| MME LEVAQUE: | No, no of course not . . . |
| MAIGRAT: | But as I say, we'll forget about that for the moment shall we . . . |
| MME LEVAQUE: | Thank you. |
| MAIGRAT: | Now, what was it? Three large loaves . . . a jar of coffee . . . |
| MME LEVAQUE: | And two kilos of potatoes please . . . |
| MAIGRAT: | And two kilos of potatoes. . . . I have to say I'm surprised to see you this morning Madame, it's always |

a pleasure of course, but when your father stopped by I imagined I wouldn't be seeing you for a day or two . . .

MME
LEVAQUE:    My father . . .

MAIGRAT:    Yes. Back from the night-shift I imagine . . .

MME
LEVAQUE:    Today?

MAIGRAT:    Yes.

MME
LEVAQUE:    What did he want?

MAIGRAT:    What didn't he want Madame . . . he bought all manner of things. Anyone would think it were Christmas, not that I should complain.

MME
LEVAQUE:    Grandad . . .

MAIGRAT:    A rush of blood to the head I expect . . . and there we are . . . *(He places the goods in front of her. She hands him the money. Just as she is about to pick up the goods, he holds onto them.)* . . . Madame . . . that twenty francs, it is a lot of money, I know . . . so if there's any other way you'd care to pay . . .

MME
LEVAQUE:    *(Unable to look at him.)* We're hopin' for new work next month, I'll have the money for you by then . . .

MAIGRAT:    *(Releasing the goods.)* As you wish Madame. Until next month then. Unless of course you have a change of heart . . .

> *Madame Levaque picks up the shopping and leaves. As she goes we hear a blare of the siren indicating the end of a shift, followed by the sound of an accordion playing. The lights change and we make out the silhouettes of street life above ground: men carrying sacks of coal, new miners setting off to work, old miners emerging blackened from the pit-head (perhaps exchanging head-gear with them), a couple embracing, barrels of beer being rolled along the street etc. Madame Levaque threads her way urgently amongst this activity. As she passes all heads turn and look*

*after her as she is clearly preoccupied. By the time she has disappeared Rasseneur's bar has been set up.*

# SCENE FOUR

*The lights go up on Rasseneur's bar. Souvarine sits stroking a white rabbit. Various miners about to go to work are having a drink alongside those that have just finished their shift. Etienne is very much out on his own.*

RASSENEUR:   Oh I'll not say Quality are not without difficulties, there's a crisis . . . but a separate rate for timberin'. . . !

CHAVAL:   We're fighting a losin' fight doon there as it is. . . ! With a' this loose earth aboot, we'd spend the hale day hewin' timber in place o' coal.

MINER TWO : He were nobbut tryin' to frighten thee.

LEVAQUE:   Negrel? Nay damn, not this time . . .

RASSENEUR:   Well I'll tell thee summat, if he goes on i' that gate, the brummel-snouted good to nowt'll over step himself . . .

LEVAQUE:   Aye, and go runnin' to Monsieur Hennebeau, brisk as you like . . .

MINER ONE : There's nowt he can do . . .

CHAVAL:   I've heard as much . . . *(They laugh.)*

LEVAQUE:   *(To Rasseneur.)* . . . the lad needs beddin' out. I were wonderin' maybe if one or other o' thy rooms were free at the moment.

RASSENEUR:   *(Beat)* Nay but both rooms are taken for once in a way. I can't help thee.

LEVAQUE:   Not to worry.

RASSENEUR:   Sorry son.

LEVAQUE:   You can bed out wit' us the night, *(indicating Catherine.)* you'll have to share mind . . .

CHAVAL:   *(Quietly)* Ach weel noo, wha's the lucky lad . . .

*Catherine finds herself caught between Chaval and Etienne.*

RASSENEUR: I heard as how there's talk of a lock-out today; some lad came over from the glass-works earlier on; a right larl rattlebones he were, wit' face as long as parson's nose, all rigged up in a pair of spectacles. . . . 'Is there no work about here' he says, so I tells him. 'What about Fauvelle?' he says, 'I were told there were some factories there . . .' 'Oh aye, there's a good few factories there', I says, 'but there's nowt in them, see. You're three years over late.' And then he told me about lockout. Wanted to know if we'd any brass . . . *(He laughs.)* . . . I gave him five loaves, he seemed well suited. Flesh, blood and bones'll rise up against it afore long, there's nowt about it.

LEVAQUE: Nay . . . enough o' that gab. It doesn't do to bite the hand that feeds.

RASSENEUR: Right, so long as it does feed.

*Chaval meanwhile has been trying to persuade Catherine to drink some beer.*

LEVAQUE: Chaval, hast tha no sense about thee . . . leave her be . . .

CHAVAL: It's only beer . . .

LEVAQUE: If she'll not drink, she'll not drink . . .

CHAVAL: I dinnae blame thee . . . this beer tastes o' rice 'n soap-suds.

CATHERINE: Dad! . . . Mother'll be waitin' . . .

LEVAQUE: Oh let her wait a while, I'll not be long now . . .

RASSENEUR: A letter came today . . .

LEVAQUE: Oh aye? *(Beat)* Well?

RASSENEUR: *(Nervous of saying this in front of Etienne.)* From Pluchart.

LEVAQUE: Pluchart!

RASSENEUR: Aye, he's back from London. Now there's a man who can hang his hat up here any time he's a mind to. If he

had his way, things round here would be put to rights
and fast.

ETIENNE: They certainly would. *(The two men turn and stare at
him.)* . . . I know Pluchart . . .

RASSENEUR: How's that?

ETIENNE: When I was training to be an engineer, he was my
foreman. The best I ever had. I often used to talk with
him about things.

RASSENEUR: What manner of things?

ETIENNE: Things that used to vex him . . . and both of us . . .

*Rasseneur is visibly impressed.*

RASSENEUR: This young lad's wit' thy team, tha say?

LEVAQUE: As of today, aye.

RASSENEUR: Hold there a moment.

*He exits for a moment.*

LEVAQUE: He's safe to help thee now son, you said the right
thing . . .

ETIENNE: How does he know Pluchart?

LEVAQUE: The last time we had trouble here, there were many a
time he wrote to him for advice.

ETIENNE: Did he get it?

LEVAQUE: Aye, marry. Like clockwork. They'd not let him down
again though. He's been pourin' beer ever since. He's a
dreamer lad, and dreamin' never took anyone any place.
Aye it would be glorious and beautiful to have paradise
here on earth, it would be Christianity itself, if it were
for the good of all, instead o' that merely one set of folk
as opposed to another.

CATHERINE: Dad . . .

LEVAQUE: Alright, I'm comin' . . . he'll have his paradise, but all
in good time. None of us'll be nowt no different up
there.

*Rasseneur re-enters.*

RASSENEUR :  It seems we've a room after all young man.

ETIENNE :  Thank you very much. *(To Levaque.)* . . . and you too . . .

LEVAQUE :  We must be shiftin' . . . Catherine . . .

RASSENEUR :  Tha'll let me know if tha hears 'owt else, won't tha . . .

LEVAQUE :  It's to no use thee askin' me, there's things tha know about in here that've not happened yet!

SOUVARINE :  I beg to excuse me my friend. I am so curious. If you only have arrived here this morning, how is it that you have no baggage. . . ?

LEVAQUE :  Look to thy own affairs. . . .

*Etienne finds himself very much the centre of attention. He holds up a small bundle he has been carrying.*

ETIENNE :  This is my baggage . . . I left in a hurry.

SOUVARINE :  Oh? . . . please, I do not wish to be prying but . . .

ETIENNE :  I was sacked from my last job.

RASSENEUR :  Oh ay . . . what for?

ETIENNE :  I hit one of the foremen.

MINER ONE :  You hit the gaffer?

ETIENNE :  Yes.

CATHERINE :  What with?

ETIENNE :  My hand . . . fist, rather. I'd been drinking.

LEVAQUE :  Well you'll have to mind and tread your toes straight here. I'm fair scared to think what'd happen if you struck Monsieur Negrel . . .

SOUVARINE :  *(Holding out his hand.)* . . . Souvarine. I am pleased to make your acquaintance.

*Etienne shakes his hand.*

ETIENNE :  Etienne Lantier.

SOUVARINE :  Ah forgive me, how impolite . . . *(He holds up his rabbit.)* . . . this is Pologne.

ETIENNE :  How do you do Pologne . . .

SOUVARINE: Oh my friend, he understands only Russian.

ETIENNE: Zdrastvuiti . . .

SOUVARINE: Aha!

RASSANEUR: When you two are through, I'll show the lad his room . . .

> *At that moment Madame Levaque enters and stands in the doorway.*

LEVAQUE: I'm comin' woman, I'm comin' . . . I'm half-way home . . . *(He finishes his drink.)* . . . nay, don't stand there and look on me i' that road. I'm all parched up! Can a man not wash the dust from . . . out his tubes without his. . . .

MME
LEVAQUE: Grandad's sat at home cryin' his eyes out . . .

LEVAQUE: I'm not that late am I . . .

CATHERINE: Wherefore?

MME
LEVAQUE: They laid him off first thing the morn, on account o' his legs . . . *(Silence)* . . . he'll not be goin' down again, never no more . . .

LEVAQUE: But he's not passed sixty! He's missed nobbut eight days in six months and . . . what by that . . .

MME
LEVAQUE: *(Quiet)* You'd best come home.

> *He marches out. Mme Levaque and Catherine follow. Etienne and the others look after them in silence.*

RASSENEUR: They'll scraffle through. They have done thus far.

> *The lights go down on the bar except for a spot on the accordion player, who plays as the bar is cleared. Elsewhere we see the community going about their various activities including Levaque being bathed by Madame Levaque, and Monsieur Hennebeau being 'silhouetted' to the sound of a violin concerto. Etienne wanders from scene to scene observing and absorbing. Eventually he reaches a desk piled high with books where he sits down and begins studying. The accordion player exits and Scene Five begins.*

# SCENE FIVE

*The Hennebeau household. Monsieur Hennebeau is seated. He is in the
process of having his silhouette made. Monsieur Gregoire stands talking to
him. He is drinking. The music continues in the background.*

M.
HENNEBEAU: There is a certain degree of unrest in the Industry in
general at the moment, yes.

M.
GREGOIRE: Is there any reason to believe that this unrest is
different in essence from what we experienced before?
*(Pause)* Can it be treated in the same manner. . . ?

M.
HENNEBEAU: No.

M.
GREGOIRE: Why in Heaven's name not?

M.
HENNEBEAU: Times have changed Leon . . . as has the nature of the
beast we are dealing with . . .

M.
GREGOIRE: Meaning?

M.
HENNEBEAU: There are organisations in existence today which will
before long have the potential to wield immense power
in our industry, a power which both you and I shall
have to take into consideration. These organisations . . .
unions, cooperative societies, call them what you will
. . . differ from their predecessors in as much as they
demand more. Far, far more. It is no longer merely a
seemingly endless increase in wages that is entertained,
but an entirely new vision of society, one that has taken
possession of the fancies of men and women alike; it is
spoken of on the house tops, whispered in secret,
published in poems, plays and songs, it has crept even
into the church, and has turned almost every head in
the country. But not this one. We cannot sit back and
allow ourselves to be trampled under foot.

M.
GREGOIRE: And just how do you propose to 'take this into consideration'?

M.
HENNEBEAU: By ensuring of course that the workforce here is sufficiently content not to request the services of these organisations. And by showing that they are in any case greatly to be distrusted, as indeed they are.

> *Monsieur Gregoire has got in between the silhouettist and Monsieur Hennebeau.*

SIL-
HOUETTIST: Scusa signor, ma . . .

M.
GREGOIRE: Mm? Oh . . . I beg your pardon. . . . I hardly think trying to maintain people in a state of content should be thought of as a problem.

M.
HENNEBEAU: I didn't say it was a problem.

M.
GREGOIRE: No, but you distinctly implied that. . . .

M.
HENNEBEAU: *(Interrupting)* Up until now, the criteria for happiness have been really quite elementary. As far as Montsou is concerned, people are beginning to get a little greedy now; more importantly they're wishing to involve themselves with matters that are not their concern.

M.
GREGOIRE: People in general or. . . . I mean what about this new fellow, Lantier?

M.
HENNEBEAU: What about him?

M.
GREGOIRE: Well a young man of his age is liable to have his hand turned by the first fashionable ideas he may encounter and I understand he's not staying in the best of company from that point of view.

M.
HENNEBEAU: True. He's turned out to be a good worker, I'm told.

M.
GREGOIRE:    Yes.

M.
HENNEBEAU:   He's also very intelligent. A man of ideas.

M.
GREGOIRE:    There's little harm in that.

M.
HENNEBEAU:   That rather depends on the ideas.

M.
GREGOIRE:    I trust Pierre Deneulin doesn't fall into this category.

M.
HENNEBEAU:   Oh Good Gracious no. There are those who choose to
             think of him as a spanner in the works. . . . I myself
             see him more as a fly in the ointment . . .

M.
GREGOIRE:    He is a good friend of mine. I should hate to see him
             disadvantaged.

M.
HENNEBEAU:   Unfortunately that is not something over which I
             personally have any control. No, the real threat lies
             with these combinations and what have you . . . the
             mob.

M.
GREGOIRE:    But surely it's not wholly unreasonable to take an
             interest in the running of an industry upon which your
             livelihood is founded. Is it?

M.
HENNEBEAU:   *(Breaking his pose.)* Do you give your servants reasons
             for your expenditure or your economy in the use of
             your own money? Of course you don't, and you'd be a
             fool if you did. Their lives are not so barren as they
             would have you believe Leon. *(He resumes his pose.)* . . .
             They have . . . freedoms . . . that you and I will never
             be able to afford. Never in a million years . . . *(Pause)*

M.
GREGOIRE:    Such as?

M.
HENNEBEAU: *(Beat)* I'm quite sure you didn't come to see me today simply to discuss the state of the Industry . . .

M.
GREGOIRE: No . . . no . . . I . . . didn't . . . *(Pause)*

M.
HENNEBEAU: It's alright you know, he doesn't understand a word.

M.
GREGOIRE: Ah. But why on earth . . .

M.
HENNEBEAU: Vanity, Leon, pure vanity. My wife's I hasten to add, not my own. I am assured it is the height of fashion in Paris. *(To the silhouettist.)* Grazie, basta por la momenta . . .

SIL-
HOUETTIST: Ma Signor, La Signora . . .

M.
HENNEBEAU: Grazie . . . *(The silhouettist leaves.)* You were saying . . .

M.
GREGOIRE: Yes, I . . . nothing too urgent. I merely thought, quite apart from anything else, that it would be useful to . . . if only to ease my mind, to clear up one or two details . . . in connection with, touch wood, the marriage.

M.
HENNEBEAU: The marriage.

M.
GREGOIRE: Yes.

M.
HENNEBEAU: Of course. *(Pause)* Well, things seem to be progressing relatively smoothly as far as I can see. What did you have in mind? *(Pause)* Leon, you do wish to discuss . . . Cecile and Paul?

M.
GREGOIRE: Yes, I'm sorry. . . . Paul more than Cecile as a matter of fact . . .

M.
HENNEBEAU: Well as I say, they appear to be well disposed towards

one another . . . but I don't really think you can rush these things . . . much as I would like to.

M.
GREGOIRE:   No, I wouldn't wish to either . . .

M.
HENNEBEAU: It's as wise to be certain in these matters.

M.
GREGOIRE:   And Madame Hennebeau . . .

M.
HENNEBEAU: . . . as certain that is as one ever can be . . .

M.
GREGOIRE:   And Madame Hennebeau, what are her feelings on the . . . affair. . . ?

*Awkward pause.*

M.
HENNEBEAU: I should perhaps mention that certain dissatisfied and troublesome elements in the community have concocted a story to the effect that my wife is enjoying some kind of liaison with Paul. I hope I don't have to persuade you of the untruth behind this accusation nor the potential damage that this kind of malicious gossip can bring about should it be granted any credence whatsoever . . .

M.
GREGOIRE:   Of course not . . .

M.
HENNEBEAU: The politics of envy are never far from us . . .

M.
GREGOIRE:   How utterly outrageous. Do you know the source of this particularly story?

M.
HENNEBEAU: *(He picks up the half-finished silhouette.)* Unfortunately not. I think it best simply to ignore it.

M.
GREGOIRE:   Quite so. Above all, we must be certain that it doesn't reach the ears of Cecile . . . or Paul . . .

M.
HENNEBEAU:  Yes. But there you are . . . these things are sent to try
            us. *(He holds up the silhouette and examines it. He shows
            it to Monsieur Gregoire.)* You see . . . there are no horns
            . . .

            *Monsieur Gregoire laughs uneasily. Blackout.*

# SCENE SIX

*Night-time. Monsieur Hennebeau can be seen standing staring out of
window. We hear the sound of cats calling to one another. Catherine and
Chaval enter into the light thrown by the window. Chaval is forcibly
kissing her. Monsieur Hennebeau watches.*

CATHERINE:  *(Breaking loose from him.)* Let me alone!

CHAVAL:     Ach wha are ye barkin' at. . . . I'll no' harm ye.

CATHERINE:  I'm late enough as it is.

CHAVAL:     Tae hell! It'll no' make ony difference noo, and I
            wouldna fancy walkin' back on my ain at this time o'
            nichts, nay no' if ye were tae gang doon on your
            bended knee . . . no' wi' the Black Miner aboot . . .

CATHERINE:  Who?

CHAVAL:     Ha'e ye no' heard o' the Black Miner . . . who drills wi'
            his nose and cuts wi' teeth?

CATHERINE:  Nay.

CHAVAL:     The auld hewer that comes up frae La Gorge at the
            daid o' nicht tae wring the necks of a' the lads and
            lassies on their ain . . . especially lassies . . .

CATHERINE:  I don't believe you, I don't believe one word.

CHAVAL:     It's troo I tell ye . . .

CATHERINE:  I have to be goin' home or Dad'll kill me.

CHAVAL:     I wouldna worry mysel' ower that . . . it's no' worth it;
            I work wi' him.

CATHERINE:  That's what I'm worried about.

CHAVAL:        Why? You dinna ha'e tae tell him onything.

CATHERINE:     I don't want 'owt . . . not to tell . . .

CHAVAL:        And there's me buyin' ye presents . . . *(He touches the ribbon in her hair.)* . . . I'm nobbut puttin' my arm round ye . . .

CATHERINE:     I know but . . .

CHAVAL:        Sht! *(They freeze.)* . . . I thoucht I heard somethin' . . .

CATHERINE:     Where? *(He puts his arm round her 'in protection'.)* . . . Oh stop it, you're nobbut tryin' to frighten me.

CHAVAL:        I wouldna frichten ye . . . nae for onythin' i' the world.

CATHERINE:     Oh aye . . .

CHAVAL:        I may seem hard-hearted frae time tae time but likely I'm only puttin' it on. . . . I can be gey kind when I want tae . . .

CATHERINE:     *(Half laughing, half frightened.)* . . . Stop it . . .

CHAVAL:        You dinnae want me tae . . .

CATHERINE:     I do.

CHAVAL:        Nae.

CATHERINE:     Aye.

CHAVAL:        Nae.

CATHERINE:     Aye!

CHAVAL:        Wha for? Dae ye no' like me?

CATHERINE:     *(Beat)* Nows and thens . . .

CHAVAL:        When?

CATHERINE:     When you're quiet. And not shoutin'.

CHAVAL:        If you're quiet, you dinna get heard. And if you dinna get heard, that's it. If a body doesna look after the'sels in this world there's naebody else will. *(Pause)* I ken what it is.

CATHERINE:     What?

CHAVAL:        I thoucht ye had mair savvy then to tak' a notion of a bookworm.

CATHERINE:  Who?

CHAVAL:  Lantier, that's wha . . .

CATHERINE:  It's not true.

CHAVAL:  Tae hell it's no'! And him mebbe movin' intae the hoose afore Christmas I hear . . .

CATHERINE:  What by it? Grandad's been poorly . . . we need the wage . . .

CHAVAL:  Grandad'll no' be the only yin wha's poorly once he's done wi' ye. Am I richt or nae?

*She doesn't answer.*

CATHERINE:  Dad said it were wrong, and that if I did . . . *(She stops.)*

CHAVAL:  What? . . . what?

CATHERINE:  I'd be punished after . . .

CHAVAL:  He wouldna ken . . . and suppose he did, he wouldna lay a finger on ye . . .

CATHERINE:  Nay, not by him.

CHAVAL:  Wha then? *(She doesn't answer.)* Ach, he's no' been fillin' your haid wi' that javver has he?

CATHERINE:  It's not javver.

CHAVAL:  What did he say?

CATHERINE:  He said I'd not go to Heaven . . .

CHAVAL:  Ye wouldna gang to Heaven . . . for kissin'!

CATHERINE:  No, not just kissin' . . .

CHAVAL:  Hoo d'ya think ye came to be alive then, or were ye found at the front-door in a paper-bag?

*She laughs. He puts his arms round her again.*

CHAVAL:  Yin wee kiss . . . and I promise I'll no' ask again . . .

*Reluctantly she kisses him. He starts steering her into the shadows at the back, out of sight. She resists.*

CATHERINE:   Nay, let me go . . . please! Let me go . . . help me!

> *Her voice is stifled. Monsieur Hennebeau watches*
> *on. He wraps himself in his own arms, clearly aroused*
> *by the whole incident. Black-out.*

# SCENE SEVEN

*Out of the blackout we hear Levaque and Rasseneur.*

LEVAQUE:   Four and a half sous per tub!

RASSENEUR:   Nay what!

> *The lights come up on Rasseneur's bar as full of as*
> *many miners as are available, all looking at Levaque*
> *who stands in the doorway. He moves to the bar.*

LEVAQUE:   Aye marry, four and a half!

MINER ONE:   Was Negrel there?

LEVAQUE:   Nay damn, he'd not do his own dirty work, would
he . . .

RASSENEUR:   That's it then, if we're aimin' to right things up, now's
as good a time as 'owt.

MINER
THREE:   What, would'st have us all standin' round at street
corners again . . . YOU should recall what happened
last time . . .

ETIENNE:   Circumstances have altered now, they're in our favour
. . .

MINER
THREE:   And how would you know?

LEVAQUE:   Aye, if I were thee son, I'd look to the bull-rush and
keep my head down . . .

ETIENNE:   Look. *(He holds up a letter.)* It's a letter from Pluchart.

MINER ONE:   Oh aye . . .

RASSENEUR:   To thee!

*He takes the letter off him.*

ETIENNE:       Yes. He knows what's happening. It's the same all over. He wants us to join the Workers' International.

RASSENEUR:     *(Handing the letter back.)* Nay, I'd as ginner join the Quality as themfolk.

ETIENNE:       Why not? They might be able to give us some support.

MINER ONE:     How?

ETIENNE:       If we went on strike.

RASSENEUR:     Aye, right well, I'm all for it but I say it again, we've no need of them in Paris.

MINER ONE:     You aim it's comin' to that road?

MINER
THREE:         Nay!

ETIENNE:       Within the week . . .

RASSENEUR:     Hark at him! It doesn't just happen . . . you need a strike fund . . .

ETIENNE:       I know . . .

RASSENEUR:     . . . you need . . . it takes plannin' and preparations . . .

ETIENNE:       I know.

RASSENEUR:     Tha knows! What does tha know, th've barely been here a month . . . tha wants to run afore tha can walk, that's thy trouble . . .

MINER
TWO:           At least he wants to run.

SOUVARINE:     Excuse me Gentlemen . . . please, but what do you hope to gain by going on this strike?

*Pause. All eyes turn to Etienne.*

ETIENNE:       Higher wages to begin with . . .

SOUVARINE:     Higher wages. For the same work? For more work? For less work? Which?

ETIENNE:       For less work.

SOUVARINE:     More money for less work. And do you think they will accept this?

ETIENNE:        No.

SOUVARINE:    So?

ETIENNE:        They'll have to.

SOUVARINE:    Why?

ETIENNE:        We'll make them.

SOUVARINE:    You have a magic wand that you will wave? Let me tell
                you my friend, wages are fixed very, very carefully.
                They must not be too high or the Company will not
                make sufficient money. They must not be too low or
                the people will not survive. They must be . . . just so
                . . . sufficient for us to eat and produce more people to
                work. But I am very sorry, it is not us . . . it is not
                you, it is not me who decide what is 'just so' . . . and I
                tell you a secret now: it is not them either.

MINER TWO:  Who is it then?

SOUVARINE:    It is . . . the nature of things.

ETIENNE:        And so you change the nature of things.

SOUVARINE:    Not by going on strike.

ETIENNE:        How then?

SOUVARINE:    Ah!

                        *Pause.*

ETIENNÉ:        Well I think you're mistaken. Listen, if all of us in this
                room decided that the beer was too dear and refused to
                buy any, Monsieur Rasseneur would have to reduce the
                price, wouldn't he . . .

RASSENEUR:   Or I could stop serving you . . .

ETIENNE:        You could but you wouldn't do any trade; yes, wages
                are arranged in the way you say they are; but that
                doesn't mean to say you can't disarrange them.

SOUVARINE:    But my friend there is a difference between six or seven
                men in a public house and ten thousand men in a coal-
                mine.

ETIENNE:        But that's it! If we joined the International it wouldn't
                be six or seven men . . . or even ten thousand . . . it

would be every working man and woman in this country and abroad. Just think of all the people! With their support we could . . . we could double our wages in . . . six months . . . or even abolish the wages system altogether.

*Laughter.*

RASSENEUR: And if everyone in't world were to jump up and down all at once, I tell thee summat, the earth would move six centimetres . . .

*Laughter.*

SOUVARINE: It would be nice if it was that simple.

ETIENNE: It IS that simple. Levaque has just been standing with five hundred other miners bidding for a contract on the new seam at La Gorge; whoever can mine at the cheapest rate, gets the job; so every time anyone opens their mouth and puts in a lower bid, they cut not only their own throat, but the throat of everyone else who's there. When are we going to begin to work FOR instead of AGAINST each other? When are we going to understand that our only chance lies in the combining together of men in one common interest? That's what the International's for . . . to help people bind together.

*Silence. They are impressed at his passion and eloquence. Chaval and Catherine enter.*

CHAVAL: Four and a half, eh? Four and a half! That's nothin' to blaw aboot, is it . . .

LEVAQUE: News travels fast.

CHAVAL: Bad news, ay. . . . What kind o' wage is that?

LEVAQUE: Yours for one. So you'd best be gettin' used to it.

CHAVAL: Tae flames wi' that! Did ye thank him for it tae?

RASSENEUR: Easy now, let it rest there . . .

CHAVAL: Weel, if I'd been there, I wouldna budged below six . . . he didna ha'e the pluck to badger and that's a' there is tae it.

LEVAQUE: *(Aggressive)* Had tha been there, we'd have three weeks

holiday hard enough, but tha weren't there, were thee
. . . tha were too busy daddlin' and gallivantin' wi'
some lass . . .

*He looks hard at Catherine. There is a dangerous
silence.*

RASSENEUR: Well it's to no good stirrin' up strife now. Its done.

CHAVAL: Aye it's done.

MINER ONE: There are those as thinks we should start a strike
fund . . .

CHAVAL: I say it's a damned sicht easier tae go oot and crack a
few skulls open.

ETIENNE: You'll still only earn four and a half sous per tub.

CHAVAL: Mebbe, but I'll feel better.

MINER
THREE: YOU'LL not be earnin' owt.

RASSENEUR: That's what the fund's for . . .

ETIENNE: Yes.

LEVAQUE: Why, you're all as bad as one another . . . crack open a
few skulls. . . . Heaven preserve us from that manner of
talk.

MINER TWO: There speaks the voice of God.

LEVAQUE: Aye, and tha'd do best to heed it.

RASSENEUR: *(To Levaque.)* Tha's so full o' the world to come, tha's
blind to 'owt else. Think man, think!

LEVAQUE: I've thought 'til my brains are past achin', believe me I
have . . .

ETIENNE: He's right. Set to work on what you see and know; the
purse and the gold and the notes . . . they're the real
things, things as can be seen and touched.

MINER
THREE: Folk were talkin' like you a thousand years since . . .

ETIENNE: It's different now.

MINER
THREE:        Why? Cos you're the one that's sayin' it?

ETIENNE:      *(Beat. He raises his right arm.)* All those in favour of
              starting a fund.

              *There is a half-hearted response. Levaque, Catherine
              and Chaval do not respond, though Catherine would
              clearly like to. Pause.*

CATHERINE:    I think it's a good notion . . .

LAVAQUE:      Much tha knows about it . . . tha thinks 'owt's a good
              notion if it takes thee from thy work . . .

CHAVAL:       I'll ha'e mind o' that . . .

LEVAQUE:      *(Very aggressive.)* I should forget it right slippy if I
              were thee . . .

RASSENEUR:    Now, now . . . calm yourselves . . . *(He motions one of
              the miners to play the accordion.)* . . . like the lad said,
              it's a sore enough time without having to fight amongst
              werselves.

              *(Pause)*

SOUVARINE:    *(As the music beings to play.)* You people . . . you are so
              good at maintaining your principles but they are not
              worth anything. All they do is to clear your conscience.

MINER TWO:    At least we've a conscience to clear.

SOUVARINE:    Oh I have one too my friend. Have no fear. But unlike
              you, I worry about what I haven't done, not what I
              have.

              *Normal conversation resumes. Levaque watches
              Catherine and Chaval suspiciously. Encouraged by
              Rasseneur, the accordion player starts a dance tune
              and gradually the tension breaks, people start clapping,
              stamping, dancing etc as the music gathers pace.
              Levaque watches on. Suddenly the door opens, Negrel
              enters. The music peters out as one by one they notice
              him. In complete silence he walks to the centre of the
              room.*

NEGREL:       There's been an accident at La Gorge. Five hours after
              the repair team went down this morning, the best part

of fifty metres of tunnel collapsed behind them. If they'd been ten minutes later, they'd still be down there now; as it is, there are no casualties. Because some of you won't take the time or trouble to do the necessary work on the timbering, because some of you think more of your weekly wage than you do of your fellow men, today, while you were dancing and drinking, six men nearly lost their lives, and I can tell you that if the worst HAD come to the worst, I wouldn't be standing here calling it an accident, I'd be calling it downright murder! *(Silence)* In the light of all this, Monsieur Hennebeau has instructed me to tell you that in the interest of your own safety, the Board of Directors will shortly be offering separate payment for timbering and a lower rate per tub to compensate.

*He turns and exits. There is complete silence. After a while, Etienne raises his arm once again in the air. Led by Rasseneur, the others follow suit, until Levaque is the only dissenter. Feeling the pressure from all sides, he at last crosses himself and raises his arm to join them. Blackout.*

*END OF ACT ONE*

# ACT TWO

## SCENE ONE

*The Hennebeau household. Chamber music. We hear a confusion of voices approaching from outside. The completed silhouette from Act One is in evidence. The door opens and Monsieur Gregoire, Cecile, Monsieur Deneulin, Paul Negrel, Monsieur Hennebeau and Madame Hennebeau enter chatting animatedly. They sit at the table and are served soup.*

M.
DENEULIN: . . . of course, I can't say it was entirely unexpected, nevertheless I'm sorry to hear the news; it must be something of a headache for you Marcel . . .

M.
HENNEBEAU: Well yes, I suspect for all of us in the long run . . .

CECILE: But what have they gone on strike for?

M.
HENNEBEAU: *(Dry)* For the mastery and ownership of other people's property, that's what for . . .

MME
HENNEBEAU: Round the other side, Leon . . .

CECILE: We'll have to take food parcels into the village I expect.

M.
GREGOIRE: Oh Cecile . . .

CECILE: We did last time.

MME
HENNEBEAU: No Paul, you're over there . . .

M.
GREGOIRE: I doubt it will last that long my dear; after all, they're a good-natured crowd at heart.

NEGREL: You seem very calm about it all, Marcel . . .

M.
HENNEBEAU: Relieved, I think is the word, Leon.

NEGREL: Relieved. . . ?

M.
HENNEBEAU: Yes, after all . . . the new . . .

MME
HENNEBEAU: Marcel . . .

>*She indicates M. Gregoire who is preparing to say
grace . . .*

M.
HENNEBEAU: Oh . . .

M.
GREGOIRE: 'For these and all thy bountiful gifts, Dear Lord above
we humbly thank thee. Amen.'

>*They sit. Soup is served.*

M.
HENNEBEAU: Yes, their strike fund is still in its infancy. Had they
been able to resist the temptation to flex their muscles
and waited several months . . . who knows.

M.
GREGOIRE: There you are, you see, it CAN'T last long. Besides, as
I say, I don't think they really mean any harm.

M.
HENNEBEAU: It's hard to tell.

M.
DENEULIN: Whether they mean it or not, they might cause a great
deal, isn't that so Marcel?

M.
HENNEBEAU: Possibly.

CECILE: We knew there was something wrong as soon as we set
out didn't we, Papa . . .

M.
GREGOIRE: Yes indeed.

CECILE: There were people everywhere . . . just standing about
on corners . . .

MME
HENNEBEAU: At least the village has come to life; maybe it's not such
a bad thing after all.

M.
HENNEBEAU: Paul, draw the curtains will you. . . ; we don't want to appear provocative.

MME
HENNEBEAU: Oh really Marcel, you're as bad as Cook. Do you remember last time this happened, we sent Cook to Marchiennes to collect some oysters for supper and would she go? Not for the life of her! We even offered her our carriage and she was afraid they might throw stones at her.

M.
HENNEBEAU: You may well laugh, but I think it's as best to be safe than sorry.

> *Negrel suddenly and dramatically pulls back a flap of the curtain.*

NEGREL: Ha ha! Caught in the act! The filthy bourgeoisie enjoying themselves . . . tch, tch, tch. What would Monsieur Lantier say. . . !

CECILE: Paul, stop it.

M.
HENNEBEAU: Yes, I don't think it's wise to make too much noise.

NEGREL: Oh go on with you all . . . you're behaving as if there was a pack of wild animals out there.

M.
HENNEBEAU: We don't want to be indiscreet that's all.

NEGREL: I assure you their bark is considerably worse than their bite . . .

M.
GREGOIRE: I agree Paul, but as your uncle says, better safe than sorry.

NEGREL: Very well. At risk of provoking a revolution then, shall I pour the wine . . .

MME
HENNEBEAU: Thank you Paul.

MARIE: Someone to see you Monsieur.

M.
HENNEBEAU : Excuse me . . .

MME
HENNEBEAU : Don't be long will you Marcel or the soup will get
cold . . .

M.
HENNEBEAU : *(Exiting)* I won't.

*Pause.*

M.
DENEULIN : So. Etienne Lantier is the thorn in your flesh, is
he. . . ?

CECILE : Ooh this is delicious . . .

NEGREL : By no means. As yet there are no thorns.

M.
DENEULIN : But plenty of flesh.

NEGREL : Every pit has its frictions, I'm sure Vandame's no
exception.

M.
DENEULIN : . . . Vendame's no . . . you won't find any of my men
standing about on those street corners; I know each and
every one of them personally. I know whether they're
married or engaged or single, whether they have two
children or twelve; I even know what they have for
breakfast . . . . why? Because we trust one another. . . .
We respect one . . .

NEGREL : . . . at the moment, yes. But the time may come when
for one reason or another they decide to sharpen their
nails . . . in which case . . .

M.
DENEULIN : But why?

NEGREL : . . . in which case it might benefit you if you enjoyed
the protection of a large organisation . . . such as the
Montsou / Mining Company . . .

M.
DENEULIN : Oh that's your game, is it. . . . I'd rather have a
threatened pit than no pit at all. No, I may be short of
brass but at least my men are with me.

NEGREL:            I admire your confidence and your pride.

M.
DENEULIN:          Then you're the only one round here that does.

                   *Pause.*

NEGREL:            *(Changing the subject.)* I presume Monsieur Gregoire
                   that you've taken the necessary precautions at home.

M.
GREGOIRE:          Mm? How do you mean?

NEGREL:            Well, you're a shareholder in Montsou aren't you . . .
                   living off the fat of the land. . . ; I would have thought
                   you'd be wise to lock . . . your doors.

M.
GREGOIRE:          Living off the fat . . . of the land!

CECILE:            He's only teasing you, Papa . . .

M.
GREGOIRE:          When my grandfather . . . bought our . . .

MME
HENNEBEAU:         He's only joking, Leon . . . Paul!

NEGREL:            I apologise. You're quite right Monsieur Gregoire, it
                   will all be over very swiftly, and what's more the wives
                   will be the ones to settle it.

CECILE:            The wives?

NEGREL:            Yes. After two weeks, they'll get fed up of having their
                   husbands sitting at home all day and send them back to
                   work.

M.
GREGOIRE:          Do you really think so?

MME
HENNEBEAU:         Where's Marcel disappeared to?

CECILE:            Well, I feel sorry for them.

NEGREL:            You'd feel sorry for anyone.

CECILE:            No I wouldn't. They do work hard . . .

NEGREL:            Don't we all . . .

CECILE:          I don't see that they should go on strike though and
                 simply not work. If everyone stopped doing what they
                 were supposed to do . . . if cook stopped cooking and
                 . . . I don't know . . . the gardener stopped gardening
                 . . . why, everything would stop. And what happens
                 then?

M.
GREGOIRE:        Absolutely my dear. Would that everyone shared your
                 common sense.

                 *M. Hennebeau enters.*

MME
HENNEBEAU:       Ah there you are . . .

NEGREL:          We were beginning to think you'd been kidnapped by
                 marauding hoards of miners' wives.

MME
HENNEBEAU:       He should be so fortunate.

M.
GREGOIRE:        Any news?

M.
HENNEBEAU:       It seems there are moves afoot for them to join the
                 Workers' International.

CECILE:          What does that mean?

M.
GREGOIRE:        Trouble, I suspect.

M.
HENNEBEAU:       To say the very least.

M.
GREGOIRE:        That's rather organised, isn't it . . . for them?

MME
HENNEBEAU:       Monsieur Rasseneur has obviously been poisoning
                 everyone with his ideas as well as his beer.

M.
HENNEBEAU:       Along with one or two others, yes. A delegation is
                 arriving this afternoon, I shall find out exactly what it
                 is they are demanding and then take the appropriate
                 action . . .

*General chitchat fading to silence. Lights down on the
guests. Lights up on Etienne, Levaque and two miners
who enter led by Marie. She exits. They stand in
silence. Suddenly a babble of conversation can be
heard, squeals of mock terror, cries of 'Hide the
cutlery' etc, as Monsieur Hennebeau enters. His
serviette is tucked into his jacket.*

I'm sorry to keep you waiting Gentlemen; you chose a
rather unfortunate day for your . . . uprising; however
the sooner we settle this business the better. *(Addressing
Etienne.)* Now, what exactly can I do for you?

LEVAQUE:  We've come on behalf of all't miners workin' for't
Montsou Minin' Company . . . well, not ALL o' them,
but . . . the major part . . . who've voted to go on strike
today . . . we're here for those as are . . . as it were.
We feel that we're unwilling, nay unable to accept the
new rate o' payment that has been introduced of late.
*(Beat)* That's it.

M.
HENNEBEAU: Well now, I'm surprised and indeed disappointed to
hear that kind of talk coming from you of all people
who've been so reasonable in the past and given us
satisfaction for many years now; it was a Levaque who
brought up the first lump of coal from La Gorge, I
believe . . . I hope it isn't a Levaque who closes that
same pit.

LEVAQUE:  Beggin' your pardon Monsieur, but the aim o' my
speakin' is to show that we're not a band of agitators
tryin' to close pits or stir up trouble for trouble's sake;
we're all steady, thoughtful men, friendly to law and
order. But you know as well as us we can't accept the
new rate . . .

M.
HENNEBEAU: I don't know.

LEVAQUE:  . . . and that's nobbut' start of it . . . the fact is that
timberin' takes up a deal o' time, much more so than
fillin' tubs wit' coal.

M.
HENNEBEAU: Which is why we're paying you for it.

LEVAQUE:  Aye, and payin' us less for each tub . . .

M.
HENNEBEAU : But the whole / idea . . .

LEVAQUE :     Now if it balanced out, that were a different matter but
              it doesn't and none of us are prepared to accept that
              . . . even if we were, our womenfolk'd have nowt to do
              with it; if we're goin' to clem then we'd rather do it at
              home than down' t pit, which is why we're askin' the
              Company not only to raise the pay per tub but to
              shorten the workin' day from ten to nine hours as they
              do in the colonies. Then and nobbut then'll we go back
              to our work. (*The others agree, congratulating Levaque.*)
              I'm sorry Monsieur if I'm speakin' too plain, but I
              can't be choice in my words as them as are happy can.

M.
HENNEBEAU : Alright, alright . . . let's look at this rationally. After
              all, you start by asking for one thing and finish up by
              asking for a good deal more. A nine hour day? Not so
              long ago you wanted a ten hour day and believing that
              to be an equitable request we accepted; it seems we
              were in error for it would appear that you have it in
              mind to work an hour less with each year that passes.
              Is there no end to this? Furthermore you say that you're
              going to lose per tub; now of course, it may initially
              appear that way because you're not accustomed to the
              system but believe me, in course of time, not only will
              you make MORE money but you'll live longer as well.
              (*They all try to speak except Etienne.*) . . . I think . . . I
              think we should be honest about this, don't you . . .
              conditions in the mines aren't changing for the worse at
              all but some of the people down there are; that's the
              real problem. Someone has been promising you more
              butter than bread haven't they; well let me tell you, if
              we had it we'd give it to you, but the plain and simple
              truth is that we haven't . . . and so these people who
              are going around promising you this and promising you
              that, they're the ones who should be blamed not us,
              because that's the kind of conduct that threatens the
              very fabric of our society, founded as it is and as it
              should be on good-will and co-operation. So go ahead,
              have your strike-fund, join if you so choose the great
              Workers' International next month when Monsieur
              Pluchart comes to see you . . . yes, I know all about

that as well . . . but don't please turn to me when you find yourselves without employment.

ETIENNE: There'd be no use in any case, you won't have any to offer.

M.
HENNEBEAU: Monsieur Lantier. I was wondering how long you would be able to refrain from entering into the discussion; I'm sorry to see that much of your former landlord has rubbed off on you; and even sorrier that you appear to be having the same effect on your present landlord.

ETIENNE: Nothing's rubbed off on me; I think for myself thank you very much.

M.
HENNEBEAU: So I hear. I am informed it was largely your idea to set up a fund for the miners. *(To the others.)* Tell me, do you think it's right that this man should appropriate other people's hard earned wages to finance his own political grievances and ambitions?

ETIENNE: Tell me, do you think it's right that the Company should take our money to finance it's own crises of economy?

M.
HENNEBEAU: Oh really . . .

ETIENNE: . . . or to subsidise the shareholders' dividends. . . ?

M.
HENNEBEAU: There's a shareholder not ten paces from here who would not thank you for that remark Lantier . . .

ETIENNE: We're not asking for thanks. We're not asking for anything . . . we're demanding fair treatment, that's all.

M.
HENNEBEAU: Are you sure that's all? Bearing in mind that last year the Company spent thirty thousand francs on new housing, fifteen thousand on pensions, not to mention the free coal and medical attention . . . is that seriously all that you're asking for . . . fair treatment?

ETIENNE: You can't eat coal. If you have to make economies then you'd better find other ways than reducing our wages.

M.
HENNEBEAU:  Such as?

MINER ONE:  *(Beat)* You could sell one o' them paintin's for a start
             . . . *(Laughter)*

M.
HENNEBEAU:  I thought you were an intelligent young man, Lantier,
             but it turns out I'm mistaken; you clearly understand
             nothing of the demands of capital.

ETIENNE:    I understand a great deal of the demands of capital;
             that's why we're here today.

M.
HENNEBEAU:  In that case you should know that wages cannot be
             fixed at random; they must be competitive in the same
             way that coal prices must be competitive and respond
             likewise to the law of supply and demand. If I were
             you I should blame the facts, not the Montsou Mining
             Company.

ETIENNE:    Ah but it's the Company that decides the facts,
             Monsieur Hennebeau, isn't it . . .

M.
HENNEBEAU:  No! It's not. Economics decide the facts. Pure and
             simple economics which have an inner logic of their
             own that will not alter one jot, even may I add, in the
             face of sedition.

                    *Pause.*

ETIENNE:    Poverty will cease to be seditious when wealth ceases to
             be oppressive.

                    *Silence. Etienne motions Levaque to speak.*

LEVAQUE:    Would I be right then in thinkin' that you reject / our
             terms Monsieur?

M.
HENNEBEAU:  My dear fellow, I'm not in a position to reject or accept
             anything. I'm a paid servant like you. I have my orders
             and my task is to see that they are carried out.
             Ultimately it is not for me to make a decision.

MINER TWO:  Who is it then?

M.
HENNEBEAU: . . . the Powers that be in these matters . . . now if
you'll excuse me . . . (*He starts showing them out.*)

MINER ONE: Can we not speak wit' them werselves?

M.
HENNEBEAU: I'm afraid that's out of the question.

*They exit. Levaque is the last to leave.*

LEVAQUE: If we could depend on a constancy o' work and get
paid a good price, why then we should be happy men.

*He exits. Monsieur Hennebeau returns to the dining-room.
We hear a round of applause as he enters and cheers from
the diners. After a moment of conversation, Madame
Hennebeau emerges and calls Marie.*

MME
HENNEBEAU: Could we have coffee next door please Marie . . . oh,
and cpen the windows in here will you . . . let some
fresh air in. . . .

*She exits. Blackout.*

# SCENE TWO

*We see Chaval and Deneulin deep in conversation. As they talk Catherine
appears and makes her way past them, taking care not to be seen, and
continues on towards Rasseneur's bar. Elsewhere Etienne is trying on a
new hat. He stands in front of a mirror looking at himself. Monsieur and
Madame Levaque set off for Rasseneur's in time to see Catherine standing
there. Etienne follows shortly afterwards. Various other miners are
already seated inside Rasseneur's. The following action takes place at a
distance from the main bar area.*

MME
LEVAQUE: Aye, aye, aye . . . well might tha stand there and hang
thy head down . . . three weeks and not a word. If I'd
have known I'd have tied thee to the back-door.

CATHERINE: I'm sorry mother . . .

MME
LEVAQUE:    Sorry's not good enough.

LEVAQUE:    He were nobbut after her wage . . .

MME
LEVAQUE:    We all know what he were after.

CATHERINE:  I tried to come sooner. I wanted to but I weren't able.
            He'd not let me go.

MME
LEVAQUE:    And why not? *(Pause. We see Chaval and Deneulin
            parting company. Chaval exits.)* Well?

CATHERINE:  He'd just . . . not let me go.

MME
LEVAQUE:    Well we don't want thee . . . so tha might as well turn
            about and walk back from where tha came . . .

CATHERINE:  Mother please . . .

MME
LEVAQUE:    Go on! *(Catherine turns to go.)* . . . grievin' and vexin'
            and right put about we were. It's not as if we never let
            thee out is it . . .

CATHERINE:  I know that, but what he wants, I have to want as
            well; and he didn't want me comin' home.

MME
LEVAQUE:    Why not? There's nowt to fear in our house.

            *Catherine does not reply. Etienne realises that he is the
            reason.*

LEVAQUE:    Soften up. She's nobbut a young lass.

MME
LEVAQUE:    Not so young any more.

LEVAQUE:    Tha should never've started all this in't first instance.

CATHERINE:  I didn't start it.

MME
LEVAQUE:    Tha could've stopped it.

CATHERINE:  I couldn't. . . . I didn't know how. . . . I don't know
            how . . . *(She begins to cry. Her mother walks towards
            her and they embrace.)* I'm so full o' shame . . .

MME
LEVAQUE: Why, what a raffle we've gotten werselves into now. I knew it weren't likely up to thee. First come first serve round here. But three whole weeks without a whisper. *(She releases her.)* I met Maigrat in't street yesterday. Nice as pie he were, full o' Christmas from top to toe; till he remembered we were owin' him. I told him I'd fetch it in next week but he'd none of it. 'Promises for tomorrow don't pay the bills tonight', he said. 'If you can't pay yourself, why don't you send your daughter round the morn and we'll see if we can't settle summat out' . . . the belly-crawler!

*We see Chaval approaching.*

ETIENNE: Don't worry. Tonight it's all going to change . . .

MME
LEVAQUE: Oh aye . . .

LEVAQUE: What time's he speakin'?

ETIENNE: Eight o'clock.

*They are about to join the others in Rasseneur's when Chaval enters.*

CHAVAL: I thoucht so. I turn my heid for yin second and she's oot. It's a gey guid thing I came here as quick as I daed, or you'd be round the back wi' him by noo. *(He moves towards Etienne. Catherine tries to prevent him.)* . . . oot o't my road, woman! *(To Etienne.)* I'm glad tae find ye here . . . the man wha's gaun tae save the world; the wise man a' toffed up tae the nines I see . . . wi' his smart new bunnit and his smart new ideas. . . ; you're no' wearin' it I see . . . is that because ye cannae get it tae fit? Monsieur Lantier, oor yin and only hope. Wha dae ye think you're tryin' tae mak' a fule o'?

ETIENNE: Nobody. The Bourgeoisie.

CHAVAL: The Bourgeoisie! The Bourgeoisie! *(He picks up Etienne's hat.)* Where did ye find the money tae pay for this then? Answer me that.

ETIENNE: None of your business.

CHAVAL: The strike fund mebbe. . . ? *(He puts it on.)* Very nice . . . very nice indeed. *(He gives it back.)* On account o'

ye I've no' worked for two hale weeks noo, and frae
what I hear the strike's as like finishin' the day as it
were then, and I dinnae like it. It may suit other men
but it disna suit me; which is why at five o'clock the
morn I'm gaun oot tae my work . . . at Vandame.

LEVAQUE:     You can't do that.

CHAVAL:      There's nae power on earth tae stop me.

ETIENNE:     If you want to blackleg / then it's . . .

CHAVAL:      Ye surely think it! Me a blackleg! Ye ken as weel as I
that Vandame are no' on strike . . . they've mair sense.

ETIENNE:     They will be soon.

CHAVAL:      That's as mebbe, but 'til then I'm gaun oot tae my
work.

ETIENNE:     You wrote your name on the paper; you were / as keen
. . .

CHAVAL:      Ay, I put my name on the paper and noo I'm ta'in' it
off. Tae flames wi' the strike. From noo on, it's yours,
not mine. *(Beat)* Or hers. *(Silence)* She's stoppin' wi'
me. Am I richt? am I richt?

CATHERINE:   Aye.

CHAVAL:      Ay, *(To Etienne.)* You'll ha'e tae go withoot for a
while, won't ye . . . *(He looks at Mme Levaque.)* . . .
ach, mebbe no'. . .

CATHERINE:   *(Grabbing hold of him and pulling him away.)* Stop it,
we'll go back . . .

CHAVAL:      Ay, let's awa. . . . I cannae stand mair o' his
nonsense. . . . I ken his kind . . . they start off wi'
wantin' a new bunnit and they finish wi' wantin' a
horse and carriage . . .

             *They exit. Silence.*

MME
LEVAQUE:     God above, I may have my weaknesses but that's not
one o' them. And a fine husband you are. Oh you
brussel about in front o' Monsieur Hennebeau without
so much as a second thought but you'll not say 'owt to
save thy own daughter . . . not so much as a

murmur. . . ; if you were nobbut half a man she'd
never be in this mess at all.

LEVAQUE:     The man were half nizzled.

MME
LEVAQUE:     So?

ETIENNE:     I'll move.

MME
LEVAQUE:     Nay he's such a grip on her now, he'll not leave her
wherever she goes. You stop where you are.

LEVAQUE:     She'll be back, hard enough.

MME
LEVAQUE:     All this talk o' tearin' folk apart . . . that'll not help us
will it?? How can folk say such things . . . menfolk . . .

ETIENNE:     (In the course of the speech, the other miners are drawn
towards Etienne like moths to a flame. By the end,
Rasseneur is the only one left at the back of the bar.) We
don't have to tear them apart, that's only talk; what we
have to do is bind together in thought and in deed,
educate ourselves so as to believe in our own strength.
Look at old grandad, he can barely write his own name
. . . why? Because he's never had to . . . because he's
never been allowed to. To them . . . he's no more than
a pair of hands, a machine for digging coal to be kept
apart from the outside world. What need could he
possibly have in learning how to hold a pen in place of
a pick? What profit is there to be had from his
thinking, when there's so much to be had from his
scrabbling at coal in the guts of the earth? Well that
was the past, it's there in the air you breathe, the soil
you tread . . . the coal you dig and God knows it
always will be . . . but NOW . . . we're beginning to
think for ourselves; oh we may still be scrabbling away
underground but that's not all we're doing. We're
growing . . . I can feel it, oh yes we're growing, we're
multiplying, we're pushing up out of the ground and
one fine morning those up above are going to wake up
and look out of their windows and there they'll see a
great harvest, a great army of men and women
springing up out of the fields and they'll tremble in
their shoes, because they'll know their time is over and

that at long last our time has come. *(Silence as they all
revel in what he has said.)* It's true. You wait, you'll
see. Pluchart will tell you tonight. It's not just me.

*Lights up on Rasseneur's bar. Rasseneur stands on the
table facing a group of miners.*

RASSENEUR:    Pluchart'll not say owt.

*Silence. Etienne walks over to the bar followed by the
Levaques. He makes his way through the miners.*

ETIENNE:      Why not?

RASSENEUR:    He's not comin' tonight. I wrote and told him not to
come.

ETIENNE:      You / did what!

RASSENEUR:    Nay, don't get thy rag out. . . . I'll tell thee why . . .
the man's a politician and a fine one . . . but he's not
clapped een on a mine, let alone set foot in one. How
can a foreigner do owt other than tangle matters about
even further.

ETIENNE:      Perhaps we should ask Monsieur Hennebeau to speak
or Monsieur Negrel . . . they're both familiar with the
area . . . do you want change or not?

RASSENEUR:    Of course I want to see things righted up but not i' the
road he's settin' about it.

ETIENNE:      You voted for the strike, it was practically your idea.

RASSENEUR:    Aye, I voted for a strike, but not this one. I voted so as
folk here and about could show their feelin's for two
maybe three weeks . . . a manner o' speakin' out, a
warnin' if tha like, but the way tha's carryin' on, it's as
if tha never want them to go back.

ETIENNE:      You strike until you obtain what you asked for.

RASSENEUR:    Why, grow up lad, it doesn't work like that.

ETIENNE:      How does it work then?

RASSENEUR:    Slowly. That's how it works. Slowly. By takin' thy
chances when and if they show, by chavellin' away at
them all the time, nudgein' them sayin' 'we want this
and we want that' and if they don't give it, tha asks

again until they DO give it, and if it means turnin' out
for a while, then tha turns out, not 'cos tha's after some
great confrontation, not 'cos tha's askin' the world,
tha'll not get it, but on account of it's a way o' tappin'
them on't shoulder and sayin'. . . 'how about us then
. . . don't forget us . . .' . . . that road, things may right
up, and tha doesn't go clemmin' in't meanwhile, see
. . . cos that's what you'll do, every last one o' you . . .
clem!

ETIENNE:     Do you really believe that?

RASSENEUR:   Aye, every word.

ETIENNE:     The gospel according to Saint Rasseneur.

RASSENEUR:   Aye, I have one and I hold to it. It doesn't alter wit'
every book I read.

ETIENNE:     Do you really imagine that if we ask politely and
behave ourselves they'll suddenly give us what we
want? Never in a thousand years! Oh yes, they'll throw
us a scrap every now and then to keep us contented,
but I've no interest in scraps and nor have the people
out there. This strike is for all or nothing.

RASSENEUR:   And what happens when tha dost win? Or hast tha not
come to that chapter yet? Dost know how to run a
mine? I don't for certain sure . . . who'll be gaffer. . . ?

ETIENNE:     They won't be, that's all I care.

RASSENEUR:   Babble and saunters! If the truth be told, Etienne
Lantier is all tha care about, cos although he hasn't the
pluck to admit it . . . HE'D like to be livin' in that nice
warm house of Monsieur Hennebeau's and HE'D like
to be the one that sits at that nice big desk givin' orders
left, right and centre.

ETIENNE:     Who wouldn't! *(Silence.)* Pluchart or no Pluchart, this
meeting will take place tonight and by the time it
finishes we will have joined the International.

RASSENEUR:   Dost think they'll listen to thee?

ETIENNE:     They have so far.

RASSENEUR:   They'll do nowt but make game o' thee. *(He moves to
the door.)* . . . tha'd have everythin' all at once. In my

experience folk as want everythin' all at once end up
wit' nowt whatsoever.

*He exits.*

LEVAQUE:       I think we'd best take thee home son.

*Etienne shakes his head.*

MME
LEVAQUE:       You'll not change his mind.

*Etienne looks at Levaque.*

LEVAQUE:       Don't look on me. *(Exiting)* I know nowt about nowt
no more, whether it be up there or down here, my
head's in such a tangle. I said all I'll ever have to say to
Monsieur Hennebeau.

MINER ONE:     You did a grand job . . .

MME
LEVAQUE:       Happen it's the last he will do.

*They exit.*

ETIENNE:       You have to struggle to survive and if you struggle
hard enough then you don't merely survive, you find
power. What's wrong with that? You can't alter
anything without power. Can you? What do you think?

SOUVARINE:     What I think . . . it does not matter.

ETIENNE:       It does to me. I want to know. I want to be certain. I
want . . .

SOUVARINE:     You want a great deal.

ETIENNE:       Am I right?

SOUVARINE:     No.

ETIENNE:       Thanks.

SOUVARINE:     You asked.

ETIENNE:       Do you think he's right?

SOUVARINE:     No.

ETIENNE:       Do you think anything?

*Pause.*

SOUVARINE:   You both think this strike is important; he thinks it can 'nudge' the bourgeois into action, and you, you think it will make them to eat out of your hand. You are both mistaken. They WANT you to strike, my friend, because they haven't enough work for you anyway and they know that you will suffer more than them. And that as soon as you are tired of suffering you will go back to the mine and you will work for even lower wages than you did before, because you will be even hungrier than you were before.

ETIENNE:     And if we don't go back?

SOUVARINE:   You will. You must in the end, and perhaps you will have sent a small ripple across the surface, but so small that only after a thousand years maybe we will begin to notice the difference. Who wants to wait for a thousand years? Not I. I will be underground for ever by then. And so will you.

ETIENNE:     But . . .

SOUVARINE:   No, no, no . . . let Souvarine speak my friend, you asked for his advices and now he will tell you. . . ; we live in a prison, and this prison has a small window and this window has bars, you know? You and Monsieur Rasseneur, you fight over whether the bars should go sideways or upwards or across or down, whether they should be thin or thick, long or short, and you do not understand. No matter what you do with the bars, you will still live inside a prison. HE tells us that if we wish to be free, we must purify ourselves, by completely transforming how and where we are living. HE tells us that we must die in order to be born, we must create by destroying . . . Bakunin! My friend, Bakunin . . . the greatest living mind today tells us that if we wish to escape from our prison, we must first destroy the prison.

ETIENNE:     What then?

SOUVARINE:   Why then there will be no Monsieur Hennebeau to tell us how to live our lives. . . . I certainly will not tell you and you will not tell me; the people will spontaneously and collectively rule themselves.

ETIENNE:     But you must have some kind of leadership.

SOUVARINE:   Tch, tch, tch please . . . leadership. . . ; only the
             people, the collective leadership of the people, the new
             people.

ETIENNE:     And the old ones, do you think they'd agree to that?

SOUVARINE:   Of course not. That is why they must have no choice.

ETIENNE:     Bloodshed.

SOUVARINE:   Blood! What does blood matter? The earth is thirsty
             for blood, to make it grow. How do you think you can
             destroy property, governments, nations . . . without
             blood? Impossible. No, I tell you something my friend,
             the revolutionary is not someone who carries the works
             of Karl Marx under his arm, nor is it someone who
             prophesies the end of the bourgeoisie from the bottom
             of his beerglass . . . the REAL revolutionary is
             someone who carries a dagger beneath his arm for he is
             both murderer and midwife.

                   *Pause.*

ETIENNE:     Do you really hate everyone and everything so deeply?

SOUVARINE:   I have always believed that the only true and worthy
             passion for man is love. If I am capable of hating so
             completely, it is because I wish to love more
             completely. Here . . . *(He raises his glass.)* . . . if you
             like . . . to Love.

ETIENNE:     *(Raising his glass.)* To Love.

                   *They drink. As they do so we should become aware of
                   shadows and figures moving rapidly to and fro. A sense
                   of commotion. The low chatter of voices.*

# SCENE THREE

*The Hennebeau household. Madame Hennebeau prepares a hamper.
Monsieur Hennebeau reads.*

MME
HENNEBEAU:   I ordered them three days ago . . .

M.
HENNEBEAU: What more do you expect from Maigrat?

MME
HENNEBEAU: You don't imagine they have vol-au-vents in Montsou,
do you? . . . least of all at Maigrat's. No they're
supposed to be coming from Marchiennes; we'll have to
have them for supper now . . . assuming they arrive at
all that is. Goodness only knows what's going on in
town; there are people positively scurrying around all
over the place; anyone would think the end of the
world had come. Everything is under control, isn't it
Marcel?

M.
HENNEBEAU: As far as I'm aware.

MME
HENNEBEAU: You don't sound very confident.

M.
HENNEBEAU: Is that so surprising? . . . If it hadn't been for
Monsieur Pluchart this whole business would have
been settled in a matter of weeks. As it is, the Board
are now beginning to make noises. Disgruntled noises.
They're going to be watching me extremely closely
from now on; if I put so much as one foot wrong one
. . . they'll be only too happy to make me the Company
scapegoat.

MME
HENNEBEAU: And if all goes well?

M.
HENNEBEAU: All goes well. It can only do me good. *(Beat)* Perhaps
even a return to Paris.

MME
HENNEBEAU: I see. *(She moves up close behind where he is sitting. She
places her hands on his shoulders.)* . . . then we must
ensure that all does go well.

M.
HENNEBEAU: Yes. *(He makes a rather clumsy attempt at embracing her,
ending up clinging to her like a small child. She uses the
sound of the door-bell as an excuse to extricate herself. He
tries to detain her.)* . . . don't go . . .

MME
HENNEBEAU: Marcel!

> *She exits. He sits alone for a moment. Monsieur*
> *Gregoire and Cecile enter.*

M.
GREGOIRE: What in Heaven's name is going on Marcel? I've never
seen so many people in my life.

M.
HENNEBEAU: Where?

CECILE: Outside.

M.
GREGOIRE: On the street, in the shops . . . everywhere.

M.
HENNEBEAU: Did they give you any trouble?

> *Paul and Mme Hennebeau enter laughing.*

M.
GREGOIRE: No of course not. I'm simply intrigued as to what's
happening.

M.
HENNEBEAU: Of course.

MME
HENNEBEAU: We're all going off to enjoy ourselves, that's what's
happening.

M.
HENNEBEAU: Not all alas . . .

CECILE: Oh, aren't you joining us Monsieur Hennebeau. . . ?

MME
HENNEBEAU: Marcel has work to do, haven't you dear . . .

M.
HENNEBEAU: Indeed.

MME
HENNEBEAU: All work and no play, Cecile would you help me a
moment . . . *(They continue packing the hamper.)* . . .
I've asked Paul to come with us just in case.

NEGREL: Yes / I hope that's . . .

M.
HENNEBEAU: Just in / case what?

MME
HENNEBEAU: You don't want him do you?

M.
HENNEBEAU: *(Beat)* No.

MME
HENNEBEAU: Well that's settled then. You can be our bodyguard
Paul . . .

M.
HENNEBEAU: There's really no need you know. If things get out of
hand, I've been authorised to call upon the services of
the local troops. It might be just the thing to bring
them all to their senses.

NEGREL: I'm beginning to wonder whether they have any.

CECILE: Oh Paul. . . !

M.
GREGOIRE: They all seemed to be heading towards Vandame.

M.
HENNEBEAU: Vandame?

M.
GREGQIRE: Yes.

M.
HENNEBEAU: Are you sure?

M.
GREGOIRE: Yes.

NEGREL: You know what that means don't you . . .

MME
HENNEBEAU: *(To Cecile.)* There we are. Thank you.

M.
GREGOIRE: I didn't think they were involved in this affair.

M.
HENNEBEAU: They weren't. Until everyone else went and joined this
wretched International.

M.
GREGOIRE:      Well I hope and trust they don't intend any ill towards
               Pierre.

M.
HENNEBEAU:   Of course not.

MME
HENNEBEAU:   Are we all ready? If we don't leave soon it'll be time to
               come back.

                    *They begin to exit.*

M.
GREGOIRE:      So we can't tempt you into coming along with us
               Marcel?

M.
HENNEBEAU:   I'm afraid not, no; as you can see, my hands are more
               than full at the moment. Will you be long?

MME
HENNEBEAU:   A couple of hours I should think . . .

NEGREL:        It rather depends on whether we're abducted or not.

MME
HENNEBEAU:   *(Exiting)* If the vol-au-vents arrive, give them to Cook
               and tell her I'll deal with them this evening. *(She kisses
               him on the cheek.)* Work hard.

                    *They exit. Negrel is the last to leave. He lingers for a
                    moment. During the following exchange we see the
                    others walking across the back of the stage. As they do
                    so they cross Madame Levaque making her way
                    towards Maigrat.*

NEGREL:        Marcel . . .

M.
HENNEBEAU:   Yes.

NEGREL:        I really do think you should consider giving Pierre
               Deneulin some protection.

M.
HENNEBEAU:   Protection against what? I can't send in the cavalry
               simply because a group of miners happen to be walking
               in the vague direction of Vandame. As you yourself
               have pointed out on numerous occasions, they're not
               savages.

NEGREL:        They don't just happen to be . . . they're going there
               for a reason.

MME
HENNEBEAU:     *(Off)* Paul!

M.
HENNEBEAU:     A perfectly legitimate one for all you and I know . . .

NEGREL:        But what do / you suppose . . .

M.
HENNEBEAU:     Please! Leave it to me.

MME
HENNEBEAU:     Paul, hurry up!

NEGREL:        Very well.

M.
HENNEBEAU:     Enjoy yourself.

> *Negrel exits. Lights down on Monsieur Hennebeau and
> up on Maigrat's as Madame Levaque enters. We see
> Paul catching up with the others who have now exited.*

# SCENE FOUR

*Maigrat's shop.*

MME
LEVAQUE:       Good day to you Monsieur Maigrat . . . and a busy
               one, what wit' all that consternation outside; why it
               took me this side of a half-hour to come over. I've seen
               nowt like it; they say there's blackleggin' over at
               Vandame. . . . I'd've gone myself if there weren't the
               supper / to be found . . .

MAIGRAT:       The answer's no.

MME
LEVAQUE:       Monsieur Maigrat . . . I were nobbut wantin'. . .

MAIGRAT:       I said no.

MME
LEVAQUE:       You don't even know what it is I've come for . . .

MAIGRAT:    I know what it is you've not come for . . .

            *Pause.*

MME
LEVAQUE:    I can't be expected to pay for owt . . . it's nine weeks
            now . . . *(Silence)* . . . It is wretched to see one's
            babbies and not be able to do to them as a parent
            ought . . .

MAIGRAT:    Other folk manage.

MME
LEVAQUE:    Not for long they won't.

MAIGRAT:    Come now Madame, you'll not be on strike for ever . . .

MME
LEVAQUE:    I'm beginnin' to wonder. Whatever happened to the
            credit you promised us?

MAIGRAT:    When did I ever say such a thing?

MME
LEVAQUE:    A month or two back . . .

MAIGRAT:    Things have altered now.

MME
LEVAQUE:    How've they altered?

MAIGRAT:    Please Madame Levaque, we mustn't raise our voice
            like that . . .

MME
LEVAQUE:    Things've worsened; and that's no call to refuse credit
            . . .

MAIGRAT:    It's not as if I've been ungenerous in the past.

MME
LEVAQUE:    Then tell me why you'll not give me credit now?

MAIGRAT:    I've a wife who needs looking after. I've enough to
            worry about without getting myself into that manner of
            difficulty. *(She looks uncomprehending.)* . . . Monsieur
            Hennebeau himself came in last week and said that on
            no account were I permitted to offer credit to anyone at
            all.

MME
LEVAQUE:        . . . exceptin' Madame Hennebeau . . .

MAIGRAT:        He didn't so much as mention his good wife . . .

MME
LEVAQUE:        I don't believe it, I don't believe a word of it . . . what
                about your promise to us?

MAIGRAT:        We all make and break promises as I recall Madame.
                Come now . . . we shouldn't get so het up over it; if it
                weren't for Monsieur Henebeau, I'd be only too
                pleased to give you a helping hand, but if this shop
                were to close down, it'd be a great inconvenience for
                everyone. We mustn't take it so personally.

MME
LEVAQUE:        And how are we to eat then? *(Silence)* . . . a single loaf
                o' bread Monsieur . . .

                *He looks as if he is about to refuse again but then, as if*
                *remembering something, stops and grudgingly accepts.*
                *He places a loaf and a jar of coffee on the counter.*

MAIGRAT:        I'd not want it set about that I were giving credit
                Madame so if you don't mind, let's just say it's a part
                of the twenty francs you paid off last week . . . the last
                part.

                *She picks up the goods eagerly without quite*
                *understanding what he has said.*

MME
LEVAQUE:        Monsieur. . . ?

MAIGRAT:        One good turn deserves another, that's what I say . . .

MME
LEVAQUE:        One good turn . . .

MAIGRAT:        Was it not you who . . . oh, children these days!
                Though she's not really a child any more, is she . . .
                *(She still doesn't understand.)* Catherine stopped by one
                morning last week. For some provisions I believe.
                Anyway I explained the situation . . . and . . . to cut a
                long story short . . . we managed to sort something
                out..

> *Madame Levaque freezes for a second. Then she turns*
> *and walks to the door. Just before she exits, she stops*
> *again, looks at the food she is carrying, hurls it on the*
> *floor and exits.*

# SCENE FIVE

*As Madame Levaque storms off, the lights come up on the Vandame pit.*
*The sound of machinery. A number of miners, including Chaval and*
*Catherine are working in the tunnels. They work in silence, gradually we*
*hear the very faint sound of a crowd chanting 'blackleg'. The miners*
*stop and listen, the chant gets louder and louder. As it does, the lights go*
*down on the tunnels and come up on the area around the pit-head.*
*Etienne, Monsieur Levaque, and a miner enter. Monsieur Deneulin*
*confronts them.*

M.
DENEULIN: What the devil's goin' on here? Lantier . . . Etienne, what do you think you're doin'?

ETIENNE: We're here because we're been told there are nearly one hundred men working in this pit.

MINER ONE: One hundred blacklegs.

M.
DENEULIN: You're quite right. There are men workin' below, just as there were yesterday, and just as there shall be tomorrow. As for callin' them blacklegs, I understood a blackleg was someone who broke a strike to go to his work. Well there can't be any blacklegs in this pit, because there isn't a strike at this pit. I suggest you turn about and go look for blacklegs some place else.

ETIENNE: We don't wish to cause you any trouble Monsieur, but work has to stop here just like it's stopped everywhere else.

M.
DENEULIN: Says who?

LEVAQUE: All of us.

M.
DENEULIN: Oh it's as straightforward as that is it . . .

LEVAQUE:    Aye, marry it is.

M.
DENEULIN:    Be reasonable, will you . . . this isn't the Montsou
Minin' Company . . . these men want to work and it's
my duty to ensure that they're free to do so.

LEVAQUE:    It's our duty to make sure they don't.

MINER ONE:    Or can't.

M.
DENEULIN:    I hope that isn't a threat . . .

MINER ONE:    Take it as you will.

M.
DENEULIN:    Now listen, if I agreed to what you're askin' we'd be
closed in six weeks and sold in seven. If that's what
you want, go ahead, tell that to the men and see what
they feel about bein' on the tramp inside of two
months.

*A deputy enters.*

DEPUTY:    They're talkin' o' puttin' out the furnaces
Monsieur . . .

M.
DENEULIN:    What!

DEPUTY:    I don't believe we can keep them away for much longer
. . .

M.
DENEULIN:    *(To the others.)* Do summat for God's sake. . . !

ETIENNE:    *(To Levaque.)* Go and calm them down if you can . . .
tell them there's no need for any of that . . .

*He exits. As he goes he meets Madame Levaque.*

LEVAQUE:    Nay damn, what's tha come here for . . . did tha not
see Maigrat?

MME
LEVAQUE:    I saw him.

M.
DENEULIN:    If this pit stops work for one day, it stops work for
ever, can't you see that?

MINER ONE: That's your concern.

M.
DENEULIN: It's everybody's concern I assure you.

LEVAQUE: Get thee home, this is no place for thee.

MME
LEVAQUE: Then tell me where is! After what I have looked i' the
face i' this here world, tell me where is . . .

*She joins the others. Monsieur Levaque exits.*

ETIENNE: Call the men up and let us speak to them; we'll see
what / they have to say about it.

M.
DENEULIN: They'll be up this evenin', you can speak to them then.

MINER ONE: Call them up now; you can hear what kind o' mood
they're in.

M.
DENEULIN: I don't give a button what their mood is. I have no
intention whatsoever of callin' them up now.

MINER ONE: Then we'll have to do it for thee.

MME
LEVAQUE: We'll drag them up if we have to.

M.
DENEULIN: Over my dead body.

MME
LEVAQUE: Willingly.

ETIENNE: Hush . . . there's no need / for that . . .

M.
DENEULIN: I'll pretend I didn't hear that Madame . . .

MME
LEVAQUE: You can pretend what you will. You can pretend we're
goin' to turn about and go home but it'll not do thee
owt good.

M.
DENEULIN: These men have a right to work just as you have a right
not to work and you can't have one without the other,
that would be chaos. *(A large roar is heard off stage.)*

... if they so much as lift a finger, by Heaven I'll have the authorities round here as fast as you like.

MINER ONE: Who's makin' threats now?

M.
DENEULIN: Aye, two can play at that game only I've the law on my side.

*Levaque returns. He is carrying a bottle.*

LEVAQUE: It's to no use ... they're too busy passin' round these to 'count o' the likes o' me.

*He holds up a bottle. Etienne takes it.*

ETIENNE: Where did these come from?

M.
DENEULIN: My screenin'-shed; so it's got to thievin' as well, has it ...

ETIENNE: *(Nervously)* Order them up, Monsieur; it will save everyone a lot of trouble.

M.
DENEULIN: I'm not goin' to give in to that there rabble ... a drunken rabble at that.

ETIENNE: Can't you see? You don't have a choice, if the men ... *(He is interrupted by a shout of 'cut the cables' from off. It is immediately taken up by others.)* Cut the cables ... there are men down there ...

MINER ONE: They should never have been down there in't first instance ...

M.
DENEULIN: Dear God!

LEVAQUE: They've still the ladders.

*A miner rushes in.*

DEPUTY: They're cuttin' the cables!

*Immediately the lights go up on the working miners beneath the ground.*

CATHERINE: They've cut the cables!

CHAVAL: What?

CATHERINE:   Run for the ladders . . .

*Pandemonium now breaks out below and above the surface. Below blacklegs run through the tunnels. Above, Deneulin turns and runs to his office. The others rush off stage except for Etienne who stands not knowing what to do. There is the sound of grating machinery. Madame Levaque enters with two miners.*

MINER A:     Where's Deneulin?

MME
LEVAQUE:     In his office.

MINER B:     The word's out Chaval led them down.

ETIENNE:     Chaval!

MME
LEVAQUE:     I knew he'd hatch up summat or other.

MINER B:     He'll be gaffer afore spring.

ETIENNE:     *(To Miner A who is preparing to light a rag.)* What are you doing?

MINER A:     What say you then, lad? If it doesn't burn him out, it'll smoke him out . . .

ETIENNE:     But you . . . what about the ladders! They'll be coming out of the ladders soon . . . we want to be there to welcome them don't we. . . ?

MINER B:     Aye!

MINER A:     Nay the ladders can wait . . .

ETIENNE:     The blacklegs won't . . .

MME
LEVAQUE:     I'd not miss the looks on their faces for owt.

MINER A:     Nay well and good then . . . *(He hands the now burning cloth to Etienne.)* I'll leave this to thee . . . *(Exiting)* Over to the ladders!

*Etienne stares at the smouldering cloth and then at the bottle of gin. It is as if he is suspended in time. He takes a large swig of gin as if to build up courage. He stares again at the cloth and then extinguishes it. Monsieur Levaque appears.*

LEVAQUE:     God forgive them, hast seen what they're about? Folk
             that otherwise'd not hurt a fly. It's as if they all knew
             what were to do without so much as a word bein' spoke
             . . . as if their whole life were aimed towards this
             moment. . . . And thee stood there wit' a half-bottle o'
             gin inside o' thee . . .

ETIENNE:     I'm alright . . .

LEVAQUE:     Alright? Tha's stiff wit' fear, daffled from head to toe
             same as me. I can see it in thy eyes and smell it on thy
             breath. What was it. . . ? 'The purse and the gold and
             the notes,' eh? 'The real things, things as can be felt
             and touched' . . . Well, if this is how you come by
             them, I'd as well be doin' without.

ETIENNE:     Well I wouldn't, not for anything in the world . . .

LEVAQUE:     They don't know what they're doin' son. Do you?

ETIENNE:     Yes! It's . . . the people . . . it's how it should be. No
             leaders . . . the collective power of the people.

LEVAQUE:     The collective madness o' the people . . . *(There is a
             huge roar in the distance.)* . . . the blacklegs. They must
             be comin' up . . .

ETIENNE:     It's the people's will . . .

LEVAQUE:     I don't know whether that's thee or the bottle . . .

             *He runs off. In childish frustration Etienne hurls the
             bottle to the ground smashing it. He stands drunkenly
             and listens to roar upon roar as each blackleg emerges.
             There is one huge roar. Etienne:* Chaval! *Catherine is
             pushed on by Madame Levaque. She is exhausted from
             climbing and covered in coaldust. Chaval follows close
             behind, accompanied by two miners.*

MME
LEVAQUE:     I might have guessed you'd be down there with him.
             Have you no pride at all? Betrayin' your own family
             like that . . . *(Catherine is too exhausted to reply.)* . . . as
             for him, we ought to throw him back down again where
             he belongs . . . *(Etienne steps forward to confront
             Chaval.)* Eighty-nine o' them and he led them down. I
             tell thee there are folk i' this world as have no good in
             them . . . nowt; folk as must be crushed and cleared

out o' the way. They may be few but I have seen that there are such folk. And this man here is one o' them.

CHAVAL: I didn't ha'e the choice. They wanted tae go doon and I couldna stop them. I tried.

ETIENNE: You couldn't even stop yourself.

CHAVAL: I tried for Chris' Sake!

MINER A: Aye we heard. Blackleg today, gaffer tomorrow, that's how hard you tried.

*Pause.*

MINER B: I reckon you were nobbut scared.

CHAVAL: Tae Hell wi' that! There's mair fecht in these twa hands than the whale of ye put togither . . .

MINER A: Happen we should find out whether or no that's true . . .

*The men begin to form a circle round him.*

MINER B: Aye, tha's been sayin' it long and loud enough. . . . I aim tha want thy jacket lacin'. . .

*As they close in Catherine flings herself between them. She strikes Etienne in the face.*

CATHERINE: Cowards! Cowards! Cowards! Have you not humiliated us enough? All o' you. Well go ahead, what are you waitin' on? Kick him, kick him now that he can barely stand on his own two feet . . . and me after . . . go on!

*Pause.*

ETIENNE: She's right, that's enough. Let them go . . . let them go!

*Catherine helps Chaval to his feet and leads them off.*

MINER A: He'll catch it soon enough.

ETIENNE: Let's move from here . . .

MINER A: And hope to God I'm there to see it.

ETIENNE: Forget about him.

MINER B: Where to?

ETIENNE:       Anywhere away from here . . . Montsou!

MINER B:       Aye, to Montsou . . . to Monsieur Hennebeau's! He's
               invited us all to dinner!

               *They go off together. As the cry of Montsou is taken
               up off stage, we see a shattered Monsieur Deneulin
               emerging gingerly to survey the damage. As the sound
               fades, we hear a frantic knocking getting louder and
               louder. The lights come up on Monsieur Hennebeau.*

# SCENE SIX

*This scene moves between the Hennebeau household and the area outside
their house. Monsieur Hennebeau stands. He holds his wife's nightdress.*

M.
HENNEBEAU:     Yes, what is it!

DANSAERT:      *(Off)* They've gone mad Monsieur, smashin'
               everythin' in sight . . . hundreds o' them.

M.
HENNEBEAU:     Where?

DANSAERT:      Everywhere, Monsieur. The deputies want to know if
               you'll call out the soldiers afore it worsens.

M.
HENNEBEAU:     Have they been to Vandame?

DANSAERT:      Men, women and children Monsieur, altogether . . .

M.
HENNEBEAU:     Have they been to Vandame?

DANSAERT:      They've destroyed Vandame . . . there's barely a brick
               left standin' . . .

M.
HENNEBEAU:     And where are they now?

DANSAERT:      On the way here . . . to Montsou.

M.
HENNEBEAU:     Very well, you can tell the relevant deputies that I shall
               be in touch with the authorities as soon as I can . . .

DANSAERT:      Thank you Monsieur.

*Once assured that Dansaert has gone, he examines the
nightdress, running his fingers over it, inhaling its
smell, enjoying the texture. As he holds it up in the air
admiringly there is a loud smashing of glass. He
freezes. Rasseneur enters moving fast across the back of
the stage. Etienne, Monsieur Levaque and a couple of
miners appear from the other side.*

MINER ONE: Why now look who it is! The revolutionary bartender
himself . . .

MINER TWO: Where'st thou scutterin' to at such a pace?

RASSENEUR: Away from thee . . .

LEVAQUE: Art tha not goin' to stay and talk to us?

RASSENEUR: I'd not waste my breathe; I'm all sickened out wit'
tryin' to make fools hear reason . . .

ETIENNE: Let him go . . .

MINER ONE: Aye, let him go jump!

*Exits.*

RASSENEUR: I don't need owt o' thy charity either; see what tha's
started? Dost think they'll stop now? Now they've the
taste for it?

ETIENNE: Why should they stop?

*More sound of breaking glass can be heard in the
distance.*

RASSENEUR: That's why! This is just the excuse they've been waitin'
on, you'll see . . . the strike's as good as over.

ETIENNE: The strike's only just begun. Look at them in there . . .
*(He points up to the house.)* . . . they're shaking in their
shoes, isn't that what we've always dreamed of?

MINER TWO: Aye!

RASSENEUR: Oh he'll warzle thee into believin' owt, he will. They're
shakin' alright . . . wit' laughter!

MINER ONE: *(Enters)* We're goin' over to Maigrat's.

*Exits.*

MINER TWO: *(Setting Off.)* Aye. . . !

ETIENNE:      What for?

RASSENEUR:    Make the most of it lad . . . it'll not last for ever. Tha'll
              turn thy head for two seconds one day and when thou
              look back, the finger'll be pointin' at thee.

              *Rasseneur runs off. Etienne is left for a second. He
              runs off after the miners. The cry of 'Maigrat's' is
              taken up en masse and gradually fades as they move
              away. Simultaneously more knocking can be heard as
              at the start of the scene. Monsieur Hennebeau
              unfreezes and continues feeling the nightdress.*

M.
HENNEBEAU:    Yes, what is it now?

MAIGRAT:      *(Off)* Beggin' your pardon Monsieur, Monsieur
              Dansaert told me you were up here . . .

M.
HENNEBEAU:    Who is it?

MAIGRAT:      Monsieur Maigrat . . .

              *Monsieur Hennebeau has found something in the
              garment. He investigates and takes out an object which
              he then holds up in front of him. It is a signet ring,
              confirmation of his worst fears.*

MAIGRAT:      Monsieur? . . . Monsieur?

M.
HENNEBEAU:    Maigrat . . . oh, leave them with cook will you . . . on
              the table . . .

MAIGRAT:      I beg your pardon . . .

M.
HENNEBEAU:    Leave them . . . what do you want?

MAIGRAT:      I wondered if I might have a brief word with you
              Monsieur . . .

M.
HENNEBEAU:    What about? Oh very well, just a moment . . . *(He
              composes himself and conceals the nightdress.)* . . . come
              in. Yes, what is it?

MAIGRAT:      I were just wondering . . . I've been speaking to
              Monsieur Dansaert about what's been happening . . .
              you know the violence and everything besides . . .

M.
HENNEBEAU: What of it?

MAIGRAT: Well the truth of the matter is Monsieur that our shop being where it is, and the mood of these people being what it is, we don't feel altogether safe; I were wondering if we might perhaps wait in your kitchen for the remainder of the afternoon.

M.
HENNEBEAU: Don't be ridiculous. What do you think's going to happen to you?

MAIGRAT: I can't rightly say Monsieur, but what with the good wife being . . .

M.
HENNEBEAU: Go home, lock your front door, and draw the curtains. You'll be perfectly alright.

MAIGRAT: But the food Monsieur, they're hungry as well as everything else . . .

M.
HENNEBEAU: Our kitchen's full at the moment I'm afraid; conceal the food if you're so worried about it. *(Pause)* Well go on. Throw them a loaf of bread if you think it will help, I'll pay for it myself.

MAIGRAT: If you say so Monsieur, it being your shop . . .

M.
HENNEBEAU: I say so, now will you please leave . . .

*At that moment the sound of the approaching miners can faintly be heard. They are chanting 'bread' over and over again.*

MAIGRAT: What's that?

M.
HENNEBEAU: Go home. *(Beat)* Go home I say and stop worrying!

*Maigrat leaves. The chanting grows louder and louder. Monsieur Hennebeau's despair mounts with the crescendo of sound until he can contain himself no longer.*

M.
HENNEBEAU: Imbeciles! Bread . . . Bread! Do you really think that's all there is to it! I'd give every bone in this body . . .

every crumb in this house to be in your shoes . . . *(In a frenzy he rips the nightdress to shreds.)*

> *In front of him we see Negrel, Cecile and Madame Hennebeau hastily approaching the house. The miners can just be heard in the distance.*

MME
HENNEBEAU: It's disgraceful! Quite disgraceful! I only hope Marcel knows what he's doing.

NEGREL: They don't exactly court sympathy for their cause do they . . .

CECILE: Should we not wait for Papa. . . ?

MME
HENNEBEAU: *(Arriving)* He'll be along in a second my dear. *(Calling off.)* Marie . . . fetch us some towels and eau de cologne please, as quickly as possible . . . *(Monsieur Hennebeau enters.)* Ah Marcel, there you are, you don't appear to have had an entirely successful afternoon . . .

M.
HENNEBEAU: Oh? Whatever gave you that impression. . . ?

MME
HENNEBEAU: It's bedlam out there. Poor Cecile's been terrified out of her wits.

CECILE: I'm alright.

MME
HENNEBEAU: If it hadn't been for Paul. . . . I shudder to think what would have happened.

M.
HENNEBEAU: Where's Leon?

NEGREL: Keeping an eye on the carriage. He'll be with us shortly.

MME
HENNEBEAU: I was afraid we'd never get through at one stage . . .

M.
HENNEBEAU: Well they seem to have disappeared for the moment anyway.

NEGREL: Marcel . . .

MME
HENNEBEAU: Thank Goodness . . .

NEGREL:     Marcel, the soldiers . . .

M.
HENNEBEAU: I've already done it Paul. They should be here any
            minute.

NEGREL:     That'll bring them to reason.

CECILE:     To reason . . . what kind of reason?

M.
HENNEBEAU: The only reason that does with men that make
            themselves into wild beasts. They may be kind hearts
            separate, but once banded together, they've no more
            pity for a man than a wolf.

MME
HENNEBEAU: Look how they've torn Cecile's dress . . .

NEGREL:     Perhaps I should go and have a talk with them.

CECILE:     No!

MME
HENNEBEAU: Don't be foolish Paul, you'll only aggravate the
            situation . . .

M.
HENNEBEAU: Yes, if we can emerge from this afternoon with a torn
            dress as the sole casualty so much the better.

            *Marie enters with the towels.*

MME
HENNEBEAU: Thank you Marie . . . at least some of you have got
            some common sense.

NEGREL:     That's better . . .

            *Silence.*

MME
HENNEBEAU: I never knew silence could sound so uncanny . . .

NEGREL:     When all's quiet, the seed grows . . .

M.
HENNEBEAU: There's no need for that . . .

CECILE:     I wish Papa would hurry up; you don't suppose . . .

NEGREL:     Your father is perfectly capable of looking after
            himself.

            *Pause.*

M.
HENNEBEAU:  A drink for anyone?

            *They all accept. Monsieur Hennebeau pours drinks in
            silence. There is a knock at the door.*

NEGREL:     There he is.

MME
HENNEBEAU:  The door's bolted . . .

M.
HENNEBEAU:  I'll let him in.

            *He exits.*

MME
HENNEBEAU:  There, there child, we told you he'd be alright.

CECILE:     I know. It's just that I keep seeing their faces from the
            carriage. There were so many of them, all jostling and
            jeering and pressing up against the glass. And the
            cracks in the window-pane . . . they ran across their
            faces and made them look as if they were snarling at
            us.

            *Negrel comforts her. Monsieur Hennebeau enters alone.*

M.
HENNEBEAU:  The soldiers have arrived.

NEGREL:     At last!

MME
HENNEBEAU:  Where's Leon?

M.
HENNEBEAU:  He's coming.

CECILE:     Is he alright?

M.
HENNEBEAU:  Yes. Yes I think so.

            *Monsieur Gregoire enters. Cecile throws her arms
            around him.*

CECILE:        Papa!

MME
HENNEBEAU:  Marcel, pour him a drink. Leon, sit down . . .

CECILE:        Papa say something. Please say something!

              *Monsieur Hennebeau hands him a drink.*

M.
GREGOIRE:    Thank you.

NEGREL:       What happened?

M.
GREGOIRE:    Maigrat is dead.

M.
HENNEBEAU:  Maigrat . . .

M.
GREGOIRE:    And that that woman Cecile . . .

CECILE:        What woman?

M.
GREGOIRE:    The one who came to visit us at the house a few
              months ago . . . to think that she was carrying a baby
              in her own arms.

M.
HENNEBEAU:  What happened Leon?

M.
GREGOIRE:    After you got out, I took the carriage on and left it
              round the corner; I was on my way over when they all
              arrived at once and started to batter on Maigrat's door.
              They didn't notice me . . . they were too busy pounding
              away with their fists, bricks, anything they could lay
              their hands on, howling all the while at the tops of
              their voices. Another couple of minutes and the door
              would have given way, only just before it did, Maigrat
              tried to escape across the roof; he almost made it, only
              someone spotted him. They left the door and
              straightaway started hurling stones and bottles, as if he
              were a common cat. For a second I thought he was safe
              but then I suppose he must have lost his grip, or else
              he was hit by a bottle. Suddenly he started rolling
              downwards, banging his head against the gutter as he

went, and clawing at the tiles to stop himself. He went
straight over the edge, landed on a wall and bounced
back onto the road, right at their feet. He must have
died the instant he struck the ground, but to look at
them . . . he might just as well have walked out of his
shop-door. I tell you, they fell upon him. And kicked.
And kicked again. I saw . . . I saw them stuffing earth
into his mouth . . . handful upon handful of earth into
a dead man's mouth! And then before I had time to
think what was happening there was a knife and they'd
torn the trousers from his body and they were cutting
. . . cutting. . . . It was only then that I saw Madame
Levaque and I realised: they were all women. The men
had gone on further into town. What was horrible was
that she was wearing the clothes Cecile gave her that
day. . . ; *(To Cecile.)* for a moment I thought it was
you.

> *Cecile and Monsieur Gregoire hold each other. Silence.*
> *The sound of the miners gets louder.*

NEGREL :     They're coming back again.

MME
HENNEBEAU : Oh my God!

M.
HENNEBEAU : There's no cause for alarm.

> *They stand awkwardly as the sound of the miners*
> *grows until it is deafening. Suddenly there is the sound*
> *of a volley of gunfire, and screams as the crowd*
> *disperses. As the last shots are heard, they mingle with*
> *a violent banging on the door. Monsieur Hennebeau*
> *motions everyone to one side. The knock is repeated.*
> *The door opens slowly and a large package is placed*
> *just inside the door, which is then closed. Monsieur*
> *Hennebeau walks cautiously over and picks up the*
> *package. He turns to the others.*

. . . my dear . . . *(He holds out the package.)* . . . the
vol-au-vents . . .

> *Blackout.*

*END OF ACT TWO*

# ACT THREE

## SCENE ONE

*Rasseneur's bar. A number of miners stand staring at a declaration that has been pinned to the back wall. One of them is reading it out with difficulty. Etienne enters unseen and stands behind them. He recites the last half by heart.*

ETIENNE: 'I declare that I am not now, nor will I during the continuance of my employment with you, become a member of or support any society which directly or indirectly interferes with the arrangement of this or any other establishments or the hours or terms of labour.'

*They turn and stare as if at a ghost.*

MINER ONE: Well, well, well . . .

*Silence.*

MINER TWO: There's one or two as've been searchin' for thee . . .

MINER ONE: Aye, tha's a nerve showin' thy face here.

ETIENNE: They think I'm abroad.

MINER TWO: It weren't them I had in mind.

*Pause.*

MINER
THREE: Three dead, and all they can offer . . . is this. *(He indicates the leaflet.)* . . . I don't know whether to laugh or cry, I'm that run out.

ETIENNE: Do you think a day has passed without my seeing them lying there on the ground. . . ?

MINER
THREE: That'll not bring them to life.

ETIENNE: Any more than blaming me. Or you. Or anyone else in this room.

MINER ONE: There are folk as say tha took fright and turned thy back; on them AND us.

ETIENNE: There are those that'll tell you the world is flat if they have an interest.

MINER
THREE: Aye, there are . . .

MINER TWO: It were thee as brought us there. It were thee as boldened us to do it in't first instance. But tha never told us it'd come to an ending-up such as this.

ETIENNE: So what are saying. . . ? The strike's over? You want to go back next month. . . ? You're thinking of going back next month. . . ? . . . You've already decided to go back next month. *(Pause. No one replies. Etienne walks over and tears down the declaration.)* The Company are as hard set as we are; more and more pits are flooding with each day that passes, and it's not only the mines that are affected, it's everything that uses coal / in any shape or form . . .

MINER ONE: We've not heard from the International for eight weeks now. . . . Rasseneur says that / Pluchart has been . . .

*Rasseneur has entered unseen to Etienne.*

ETIENNE: Rasseneur says! If you listened to everything he said you'd be digging coal at one sou per tub for the rest of your lives.

RASSENEUR: Aye, and thy landlord 'd be alive yet . . . think on that! He's right, Pluchart has written. To me. It seems they've the same problem down there as we have up here; namely folk have got into the management of things, see . . . as were either fools or not true men. You should never go against the law o' the land. When you know you're right in your demand, you don't want to have right all mixed up wit' wrong, so as folk can't separate it. Now have the courage to say it, the strike's as dead as if those soldiers had made it four instead o' three. You've failed, every last one o' you.

ETIENNE: I'll not say it! Never! Even if we were all to return tomorrow morning.

MINER
THREE:            *(Aggressive)* Tha's had our blood, what more dost want?
                  I don't want to look back in thirty years and say, well
                  I've had a right miserable life I have but leastways
                  I've made some other body happy, even though he
                  mayn't yet be born . . .

RASSENEUR:        *(Protecting Etienne from the others.)* Alright, easy
                  there . . .

                  *(Pause)*

ETIENNE:          No matter what has happened or what will happen . . .
                  no matter what you or anyone else says . . . it's better
                  to light a candle than forever sit in the dark.

RASSENEUR:        Hark at him! the same old fancy words. Half thy
                  trouble is that folk can't make end nor side of owt tha
                  raffle on about. *(To the others.)* If you'd nobbut heeded
                  me at the outset, every one o' you, things might've
                  ended up different. Well I'm not going to stand here
                  and crow over that . . . but you've a chance now to
                  make an end of all this, so grasp it wit' both hands.
                  I've seen enough blood and hunger for one lifetime.

                  *Chaval enters with Catherine.*

CHAVAL:           Rasseneur! Pu' the cork will ye! *(Silence)* Ay, I kent
                  you'd be richt glad tae see me. . . ; fill up a guid stiff
                  glass will ye . . . I want tae drink a richt guid health tae
                  ye a' . . . *(He sees Etienne but chooses to ignore him. To
                  the others:)* Dinna bother your heids ower me, I'll no'
                  keep ye frae enjoyin' yoursels. I see you've a gey
                  important visitor . . . *(They start talking again but
                  Chaval interrupts.)* . . . she didna want me tae come
                  doon here . . .

CATHERINE:        Please . . .

CHAVAL:           . . . she was feart I'd lose my rag . . . the most
                  unpopular body in Montsou? He'll no' be served! What
                  she disna ken is that I dinna care a damn, no' noo no'
                  then, and what's mair, she's wrang. . . . I'm no' the
                  most unpopular body in Montsou, why he's sittin'
                  here in this same room. So if he can sit and talk face tae
                  face ower the table wi' men as by every richt should be

his mortal enemies, I think the least I can dae is ha'e myself a wee dram. But dinna vex yoursels, we'll no' stay ower lang . . .

CATHERINE:    *(To Rasseneur.)* I don't want one.

CHAVAL:       Fill her up man, fill her up.

CATHERINE:    I don't want one!

CHAVAL:       *(To Rasseneur.)* And I dinna ken why YOU'RE lookin' so hot and bothered; I only daed what you've been tellin' everyone tae dae for the last three months . . .

RASSENEUR:    *(Handing them the drinks.)* There's ways and ways o' doin' things . . .

CHAVAL:       Ach it's a' the same in the end, that's wha' counts . . . *(He passes Catherine a glass.)* . . . get this ower your neck . . . *(She hesitates.)* . . . drink you, or I'll warm your ear for ye! *(She takes a sip.)* . . . that's better . . . *(Wanders over to the others.)* . . . three deid, eh . . . three deid. I ken yin or twa wha'll no' be sleepin' the nicht and no' just them as pulled the trigger. They should ha'e cried the strike off lang afore it came tae that . . .

RASSENEUR:    Just drink thy fill and leave us.

CHAVAL:       That's what I'm dain . . . am I no' permitted to talk the while? It's no' every day a man can celebrate . . . *(Pause)* . . . you're supposed tae ask me what I'm celebratin' but seein' as you're no' gaun tae, I'll tell ye and save ye the effort; when I go tae my wark next month at Montsou I'll no' be gaun as a hewer, but as a gaffer . . . *(Pause)* Are ye no' gaun tae congratulate me?

ETIENNE:      Gaffer or not you'll be on your own.

CHAVAL:       Oh so you've no' lost your gab ata', you ay ha' plenty o' that. . . . I'll be on my ain, eh? There are at least twa men in this room will be gaun doon wi' me, and just in case they or ony others decide tae change their minds between noo and then, Negrel's ta'en on twa hunner' Belgian hands, so go scrape thy tongue some place else. It a' goes tae show that some folk ha'e mair gab than sense . . . beware o' thae kind every time . . . *(No one responds. He is obviously telling the truth.)* . . .

ay lads! A few weeks wark'll put us on oor feet again,
you can be shair o' that; here's tae ye a' then . . . tae
the end o' the strike . . . *(To Etienne.)* and most of a',
tae the end o' ye!

*Before he can drink. Etienne hurls himself at Chaval.
They fight, locked together, Rasseneur and the others
try to separate them but it is impossible. They decide to
let them fight it out, Eventually Etienne gets the better
of Chaval but is restrained by the others from taking it
further. Chaval staggers to his feet.*

CHAVAL:      You needn't ha'e stopped him! He's only half a man
             . . . he'd no' ha'e the pluck to mak' an end o' me . . .

ETIENNE:     Get out! Get out of here!

             *Catherine, unsure who to support, goes to help Chaval.*

CHAVAL:      Don't vex yoursel', I'm gaun. . . ; tak' your hands off
             o' me woman. . . . I dinna want tae see ye nae mair. Go
             on, he's a' yours, that's what you've ay wanted, weel noo
             you can ha'e him. But if ever you come aboot my hoose
             again, I'll swing for ye, so help me God, I'll crush the
             life oot o' ye . . .

             *He turns and exits.*

RASSENEUR:   *(To Catherine.)* Take thy chance. Go home afore he
             changes his mind. *(Indicating Etienne.)* . . . take him
             wit' thee and mind tha keep him there. There's allus
             trouble where he goes.

             *He shows them out. Catherine helps Etienne. The
             action moves to just outside the bar.*

ETIENNE:     You should go home.

CATHERINE:   I can't.

ETIENNE:     Why not?

CATHERINE:   Mother. She were so put about when I went. She
             won't want me back now.

ETIENNE:     Of course she does. Now more than ever. *(Pause)* Do
             you hate me so much now that you won't go back?

CATHERINE:   I don't hate thee.

ETIENNE:     Why not? I killed your father.

CATHERINE: Don't say that.

ETIENNE: That's what they're saying . . . why not you?

CATHERINE: 'Cos . . . cos it's not true. When a man gets mad and angry . . . happen he does things in his passion he'd be glad to forget . . . even though he might start out with the best will i' the world.

> *Pause.*

ETIENNE: Go home.

CATHERINE: I don't know what HE wants . . .

ETIENNE: *(Beat)* What a waste. *(He moves towards her.)* You and I could have got on so well together.

CATHERINE: Aye . . . aye . . . we could. But it's too late now. It's all . . . twisted about now. *(Unseen to both of them, Souvarine appears in the background and watches them.)* . . . I must be going'.

ETIENNE: But where? You heard what he said. Think about what YOU want . . .

CATHERINE: I don't deserve 'owt else. Any road, who'll have me now?

ETIENNE: Is that how you see it? Him or nobody?

CATHERINE: Nay, him or everybody . . .

> *She runs off. Souvarine approaches. He is unusually restless.*

SOUVARINE: My friend . . . you are still bleeding . . .

ETIENNE: It's nothing.

SOUVARINE: No, no let me . . . *(He takes out a handkerchief and dresses Etienne's wound as he speaks).* Chaval, the others . . . they are all the same, you know . . . they are all cowards. . . ; none of them have the will to be strong.

> *Etienne grimaces.*

SOUVARINE: I'm sorry.

ETIENNE: Where's Pologne?

SOUVARINE: Oh . . . she has gone.

ETIENNE:     Gone where?

SOUVARINE:   *(Shrugs and laughs.)* The people are hungry. *(Pause)*
             Yes, even my comrades in Russia, who once upon a
             time made Europe tremble . . . even they are . . . oh,
             never mind . . . *(He finishes the dressing.)* Here . . . you
             see these hands . . . *(He holds them out. They are
             covered in Etienne's blood)* . . . I should like to take hold
             of the whole world in these hands and crush it to little
             pieces; then we could begin all over again.

ETIENNE:     I wish I was as certain of things as you are.

SOUVARINE:   My friend, there is no pleasure to be found in being
             certain of the sickness of the world in which you live.

ETIENNE:     No pleasure perhaps, but it must help you in what you
             do. The conviction. *(Beat)* That day the soldiers
             arrived, as I stood there surrounded by all these people
             I thought I knew, I looked around and suddenly
             realised I couldn't recognise anyone . . . not a single
             person. All I could see was this blind, unthinking
             monster, lumbering nearer and nearer towards the
             bayonets, trampling everything in its path. And I hated
             it. I hated them. Every last one of them.

SOUVARINE:   And still do?

ETIENNE:     *(Dismissive)* No . . .

SOUVARINE:   No? And yet . . . you talk now of 'they' instead of
             'we'. . . *(He laughs.)* The revolution is not that simple
             my friend. It is not that clean. It is not like turning the
             pages of a book. *(Pause)* What will happen now my
             friend?

ETIENNE:     I don't know. Some will go back. Some won't.

SOUVARINE:   And you?

ETIENNE:     No.

SOUVARINE:   Not even for her?

ETIENNE:     Who?

SOUVARINE:   Catherine.

             *Etienne does not reply.*

SOUVARINE: Did I ever tell you how my wife died?

ETIENNE: Who?

SOUVARINE: In Russia.

ETIENNE: Your wife?

SOUVARINE: Yes. You see our plans went wrong. We spent fourteen days hiding in a hole in the ground, tearing the soil from beneath the railway line; but we were given bad information, and instead of the Imperial train it was an ordinary passenger train that blew up; eighty-seven people were killed. Annushka used to bring us food in the hole, she even lit the fuse because we did not think they would suspect a woman. They arrested her six days later. Every day after that, I followed the trial, hidden amongst the crowd listening to every word that was spoken. Twice I almost shouted out and leaped over their heads to join her. But it would have been no use. One man less is one soldier less and I could tell that each time her eyes met mine she was saying no. On her last day, in the public place, I was also there right at the back; she was the fifth in turn. Only because it was raining the rope kept breaking over and over again; they took twenty minutes to hang the first four. She could not see me at first so I stood on a large stone and stared at her until she caught sight of me. And from that moment on our eyes never left each other, even after the floor was removed from beneath her feet and her body was left dangling in mid-air, her eyes continued to stare into mine. And it wasn't until the wind turned her head to one side that I was able to wave my hat and walk away. That was her punishment for lighting the fuse, and our punishment for loving each other too much. Now I know her death was a good thing, her blood will inspire heroes and heroines in years to come; and for me . . . I have no weaknesses left in my heart, nothing at all . . . no family, no wife, nothing that will make my hands shake on the day when they most need to be steady. I am telling you this my friend, because I will not have another chance to tell you. I'm going away.

ETIENNE: Where? Why, have they said anything or . . .

SOUVARINE:   No, no . . . they have nothing to say to me. I have
             asked to leave . . .

ETIENNE:     Where are you going?

SOUVARINE:   I don't know.

ETIENNE:     When are you leaving?

SOUVARINE:   Soon. Next week, maybe next month . . .

ETIENNE:     But I'll see you again . . .

SOUVARINE:   No, I don't expect so . . .

             *Silence.*

ETIENNE:     But . . .

SOUVARINE:   Tch, tch, tch . . . there is nothing else to say. *(He offers
             his hand.)* Goodbye my friend.

ETIENNE:     Goodbye.

             *Souvarine turns and leaves. Etienne is left on his own. As
             he stands there we hear the sound of merry post-dinner
             conversation, music and people dancing. Blackout.*


# SCENE TWO


*Lights up on the Gregoire household. Monsieur Gregoire and Madame
Hennebeau are dancing as are Cecile and Negrel. Monsieur Hennebeau,
rather the worse for drink, watches as does Monsieur Deneulin. The dance
ends and they all applaud. Monsieur Gregoire bangs the table with a fork.*

M.
GREGOIRE:    Ladies and Gentlemen. . . . I propose the health of the
             bride and bridegroom to be . . .

             *A chorus of 'hear hears' etc. They all raise their
             glasses and drink before returning to their
             conversations.*

MME
HENNEBEAU:   Cecile . . . I don't think you're supposed to drink to
             yourself.

CECILE: I didn't, did I? Oh dear, I hope that isn't bad luck.

NEGREL: Decidedly not. Any wife of mine shall drink as freely and as frequently as she pleases.

M. GREGOIRE: ANY wife of yours? Are you proposing to have several. . . ?

CECILE: No he's not!

NEGREL: Correction. My wife shall drink as freely and as frequently as she pleases.

CECILE: Ah but I'm not your wife yet . . .

NEGREL: I give in . . .

M. HENNEBEAU: Let's hope she has no cause to.

MME HENNEBEAU: What, dear?

M. HENNEBEAU: Drink.

MME HENNEBEAU: Ah.

M. GREGOIRE: Madeleine, while we're on the subject, could you bring in some more wine please . . .

MME HENNEBEAU: More wine! What are you trying to do Leon, poison us?

M. GREGOIRE: I hope that isn't a comment on the quality of the wine.

MME HENNEBEAU: Not all all.

M. HENNEBEAU: Yes, stop complaining my dear; it's not as if there's a shortage of things to celebrate . . . isn't that so Pierre. . . ?

M. DENEULIN: Quality not quantity, I always say.

*Negrel rises to his feet.*

NEGREL:   Ladies and Gentlemen, your attention please. I don't
          wish for a moment to distract or detract from the
          principle reason that we are gathered here, namely the
          proposed wedlock between myself and Cecile . . . at the
          same time, however, it does seem to me to be too good
          an opportunity to miss. I am reliably informed that last
          Monday forty per cent of all available hands returned
          to work *(Cheers)* . . . and I hope I'm not displaying a
          lack of caution in predicting that next Monday, that
          figure will have doubled. *(Applause).* . . . However,
          heartening as that may be, it is not the intended subject
          of my toast. No, the fact that I am in any position to
          say what I have just said is largely due to the
          experience, skill and perseverance of one man . . . to
          whom, I am happy to say, it was announced yesterday
          that in recognition of his contribution to resolving the
          situation, the Powers that Be are intending to award
          membership of the Legion of Honour! *(Congratulations)*
          . . . Ladies and Gentlemen . . . *(Lifting his glass.)* . . .
          Monsieur Marcel Hennebeau . . .

          *They all raise their glasses amid bravoes etc.*

M.
GREGOIRE: May I just add to that, all of which I wholeheartedly
          agree with, we never again want to see the tragic events
          and the violence that took place in this town some
          months ago and which I certainly alas shall never be
          able to erase from my memory. Order has been
          restored, quite properly, but I think now that everyone
          or at least nearly everyone is in unity again, it is up to
          all of us to go out and where possible heal the wounds
          that have been opened up so savagely and so . . .
          needlessly. Montsou was wont to be proud of her
          workers, in Heaven's name let's hope that we can find
          that pride again.

          *Serious hear, hears all round, followed by a brief,
          respectful silence.*

CECILE:   Coffee! Who'd like coffee. . . ? *(They all say yes.)* . . .
          Monsieur Hennebeau?

MME
HENNEBEAU: Oh Cecile, just because he's been awarded the Legion of
Honour doesn't mean to say you can't call him Marcel;
he's almost your father-in-law.

M.
HENNEBEAU: Yes indeed. . . . I'd prefer some more wine myself . . .
*(Laughter)* but I'm sure I can swallow a coffee as well
. . .

MME
HENNEBEAU: Marcel! I don't know what's come over him. . . ; don't
be so vulgar.

CECILE: Monsieur Deneulin?

M.
DENEULIN: Mm?

CECILE: Coffee?

M.
DENEULIN: Oh please.

*The others continue chatting as Cecile exits.*

M.
GREGOIRE: Oh come on Pierre . . . stop looking so miserable. It's
not the end of the world you know.

M.
DENEULIN: It's the end of mine. Betrayed on both sides.

M.
GREGOIRE: It would have had to happen sooner or later. I'm only
sorry it happened the way it did.

M.
DENEULIN: Do you know they barely gave me enough to pay off
my creditors . . .

M.
GREGOIRE: Why didn't you ask for more?

M.
DENEULIN: . . . ask for more. . . . I'd not a leg to stand on! I'd no
power to bargain whatsoever. I were relyin' on their
sense of decency.

M.
GREGOIRE:       A dangerous thing to do. Forget about the past and
                look forwards. At least you have a position.

M.
DENEULIN:       Third in command at the pit I used to own. By Heaven
                there's salt in the wound for you.

M.
HENNEBEAU:      Third in command is better than no command at all.

M.
DENEULIN:       I were never one for small mercies.

MME
HENNEBEAU:      I never asked you Pierre, how are the children?

M.
DENEULIN:       Goin' on nicely thank you . . . bearin' up . . .

MME
HENNEBEAU:      And is Marie-Anne still wanting to be a painter . . .

                *Cecile enters with the coffee, helped by Madeleine.*

CECILE:         Coffee everyone. *(Appreciative response.)*

NEGREL:         By the way Marcel, are any steps being taken to
                prevent the principal agitators from returning to work?

M.
HENNEBEAU:      Not immediately no, but in good time. And with
                discretion of course . . . discretion Paul, it makes all the
                difference . . .

NEGREL:         Yes. And punishment?

M.
HENNEBEAU:      They will find the natural punishment of their conduct
                in the difficulty they will meet in securing further
                employment. The culprits are well known to me.

M.
GREGOIRE:       Have they found Lantier yet?

M.
HENNEBEAU:      Who?

NEGREL:         Lantier, no. I believe they think he's somewhere in
                Belgium.

MME
HENNEBEAU: An excellent place for him.

M.
GREGOIRE: An extraordinary fellow.

NEGREL: Yes.

M.
GREGOIRE: You know I think he probably saw himself as the first
working man in parliament, the scourge of the so-called
upper-classes . . .

NEGREL: Yes, an idealist if ever I saw one.

M.
DENEULIN: I rather liked him.

MME
HENNEBEAU: Oh Pierre.

M.
DENEULIN: No, I did. He were honest. He may have been wrong-
headed. Dangerous even. But he were honest, and that
counts for summat in this day and age.

M.
HENNEBEAU: Hear, hear . . .

MME
HENNEBEAU: Really, you two . . . you only had to mention the name
of Etienne Lantier in this house two months ago and
Marcel turned positively purple . . .

*Monsieur Hennebeau gets to his feet.*

M.
HENNEBEAU: I'd like to propose another toast.

*They laugh at his drunkeness.*

MME
HENNEBEAU: Sit down and stop making a fool of yourself.

M.
HENNEBEAU: I'm not making a fool of anyone my dear, I simply
want to make another toast . . . what's wrong with that;
good gracious me, Paul's made one, Leon's made one

... *(The others urge him on.)* ... thank you ... thank
you. ... I hope you've all kept a small drop of wine at
the bottom of your glass; if not Cecile, I'm sure, will
oblige us with another bottle ...

MME
HENNEBEAU: Get on with it.

M.
HENNEBEAU: I'm getting there. ... I'm getting there ... it doesn't
do to rush these things ... *(He picks up his glass.)* ...
we've talked about the beginning of a new life for Paul
and Cecile, and we've talked also about the end of a
terrible strike that has dragged on for almost four
months ... both admirable subjects of a toast. But I
should like to propose another toast to what in my
opinion is an even more worthy subject, to another end
as it happens, as opposed to a beginning; in this
instance the end ... *(He pauses.)* of the particularly
sordid, deceitful and ... humiliating liaison that has
been taking place for the last year between my wife and
my nephew. *(Dead silence.)* ... thank you, so I / ask
you to raise ...

MME
HENNEBEAU: You've drunk too much Marcel; I suggest you sit down
immediately.

M.
HENNEBEAU: Sit down? But I've only just stood up, haven't I ...
haven't I only just stood up? ... and we haven't drunk
the toast yet, have we. Aren't you going to ...

*She grabs hold of him and trys to pull him down.*

MME
HENNEBEAU: Sit down!

*He pushes her off roughly. Cecile bursts into tears. The
rest are speechless.*

M.
HENNEBEAU: Don't ever tell me what to do again in your life! So ...
*(Raising his glass again.)* ... to the end of the sordid,
deceitful and ... what was it? Ah yes, the humiliating
liaison between my wife and my nephew.

*He drinks. Blackout.*

# SCENE THREE

*Lights up on a miner. He is crouched down the pit and methodically cutting away at something. He makes a slow grating sound. We cannot see who it is. Lights up on the Levaque household, lit by candlelight. Etienne is placing a number of household items onto a cloth spread out on the table in front of him. He picks up the cuckoo clock, holds it up and places it on the cloth. His actions should mirror those of Mme Hennebeau packing her hamper in Act Two. Madame Levaque watches him silently seated in a rocking chair. Elsewhere, we see Catherine gingerly making her way towards them. As she walks above, past the miner she stops and pauses without seeing him. He likewise stops and listens. We see now that it is Souvarine. Catherine continues on her way to the Levaque household and the lights on Souvarine fade. She enters.*

MME
LEVAQUE: Afore tha takes another step, just tell me whether or no that man is bound to come racin' in here and drag thee away again . . . *(Catherine shakes her head.)* . . . is that for sure? *(She nods.)* . . . because if he is, tha may as well step out now . . .

CATHERINE: He'll not be comin'.

MME
LEVAQUE: *(Pause)* Then come kiss thy mother. *(Catherine moves forward. They embrace.)* . . . what's this? *(She sees the bruises on her face.)* . . . what's he done to thee?

CATHERINE: Oh it's nowt, really it's nowt . . .

MME
LEVAQUE: We should've thrown him back that day, back down where he belongs. *(Pause)* Go and say hello to Grandad. *(Catherine exits.)* So. He's given her the go-by at last has he; thank the Lord! I thought I'd lost the two o' them. . . ; they buried him the day after. Not one o' the Quality came. Not one. I reckon they didn't think it fit for a miner to lay down his life. I don't know why; that's what folk call fine and honourable in a soldier. I thought I'd run out o' tears by the time it came to sidin' him by; but then I saw our Catherine there, cryin' her eyes out all on her own. She were standin' leant over the grave. When she looked up, I caught her eye; she looked as if she'd lived a lifetime

already. Just as they finished with all the earth and
that, she started bleeding'. . . blood all over her dress,
and I thought God above, they must have got her as
well and she's not told anyone. But they hadn't, she
weren't even there that day. . . ; she'd just . . . come on.
Funny i'nt it . . . wit' her own father lyin' there, she
comes on for the first time. I cried then. *(Catherine re-
enters.)* . . . well?

CATHERINE:  He barely knows me. Can we not have the doctor stop
by?

MME
LEVAQUE:  It's not for want o' medicine he's taken to his bed.

CATHERINE:  Can next door not help?

*Madame Levaque laughs.*

MME
LEVAQUE:  He's been down for nearly four weeks without anyone
knowin'. Wraps his face in a long grovet so as no one'll
recognise him, only I did. I didn't bury my man so as
the likes o' him could get rich. Help from next
door. . . . I'd not let them near this house.

CATHERINE:  *(To Etienne.)* What happens to the strike now?

ETIENNE:  I wish I knew.

MME
LEVAQUE:  Tha's not allowed to say that, make out as tha does
know!

ETIENNE:  But I don't. *(To Catherine.)* They're bringing in
soldiers to protect those who work.

MME
LEVAQUE:  That must be the army tha were talkin' about is it . . .
the 'great army o' men springing up out o' the soil'
. . . a new order, a new life, a new everythin' . . . that's
the one is it? Where's thy harvest now then?

ETIENNE:  Please, not you as well . . .

MME
LEVAQUE:  Aye me as well. Why should I be different? Still, now
I've come thus far, I'll not go back, less nor ever now
that he's gone. Nay damn, there are some as say we

went too far that day, I say we didn't go far
enough . . .

ETIENNE: *(To Catherine.)* They've even offered to pay from the
start of last week.

CATHERINE: But that's almost ten francs.

ETIENNE: Yes.

CATHERINE: For nowt . . .

MME
LEVAQUE: For nowt! *(She laughs.)*

CATHERINE: I didn't mean it like that. But ten / francs now . . .

MME
LEVAQUE: For nowt!

CATHERINE: Twenty francs if I / work'd this week . . .

MME
LEVAQUE: Nay! We'll have no more blackleggin' i' this family.

CATHERINE: But mother, don't you see . . . there are more down
than up . . ./. . . how long can we last like this, not
knowin'. . .

MME
LEVAQUE: It's not numbers that make a blackleg. It's what you
do. Hast tha not learned owt at all child?

CATHERINE: But it's over . . . there IS no strike.

MME
LEVAQUE: We've wrought hard for months and more . . .

CATHERINE: *(To Etienne.)* Tell her . . .

MME
LEVAQUE: *(Covers her ears.)* I won't hear it . . .

CATHERINE: What's the matter with her? We can't live on nowt . . .

MME
LEVAQUE: Least of all from him.

CATHERINE: We'd have to move . . . away from Montsou . . .

MME
LEVAQUE: We've broken the heart of it now . . .

CATHERINE:    Say summat to her!

ETIENNE:      I don't know . . .

MME
LEVAQUE:      There's nowt to be said . . .

CATHERINE:    It's not just thee we're frettin' after.

MME
LEVAQUE:      We've lasted four months, we'll last another four . . .

CATHERINE:    Mother . . .

MME
LEVAQUE:      Did HE send thee?

CATHERINE:    Who?

MME
LEVAQUE:      Him. Chaval. Did HE send thee with all this?

CATHERINE:    She's not well . . .

MME
LEVAQUE:      I'm as well as any and I tell thee this; if ever tha set so
              much as one foot down that mine, I will renounce thee.
              I shall so dismiss thee from this house, that tha'd have
              better been born motherless from thy cradle. And if
              after, tha were to come into this darkened room to look
              upon me lyin' dead, why when tha came near me, if I
              could make it, my body should bleed.

              *The lights fade on this scene and come up on
              Souvarine. He is still down the mine sawing but now in
              a different position. The lights fade on him and come
              up again on the previous scene.*

ETIENNE:      What are you doing? *(Silence)* Catherine!

CATHERINE:    I have to.

              *Silence.*

ETIENNE:      She needs you here . . .

CATHERINE:    She needs food more than she needs me.

              *Pause.*

ETIENNE:      HE'll be there.

CATHERINE:   So? *(She continues preparing.)* I'm sorry.

             *She sets off.*

ETIENNE:     Wait! Wait there . . . I'm coming with you . . . *(He starts changing.)*

CATHERINE:   Thee! *(Etienne rapidly dresses. Catherine walks slowly back.)* There's no tie / for thee to go.

ETIENNE:     I want to. Come on, we'll be late . . .

             *They exit.*


# SCENE FOUR


*The light now grows as dawn breaks. As various miners make their way to work we see the whole community at once: Monsieur Gregoire at breakfast, Cecile sitting on her own, Madame Levaque still in her chair, Monsieur Hennebeau watching his wife preparing to go out, Rasseneur at his bar. Etienne and Catherine thread their way to work. Souvarine appears, recognises Etienne and is about to stop him when he sees Catherine. Instead he turns and makes his way centre stage where he stands, his arms raised high holding the saw. All the while not only the light but also the different noises from all this activity have been growing louder and louder. Now the sound of grinding machinery takes over, drowning everything else. It becomes deafening. Suddenly Souvarine drops his arm. There is silence. Everyone freezes. After a few seconds there is a flash of white light and alarm bells/sirens begin to blare simultaneously. After a few more seconds, the men run from the stage leaving the women isolated, each in their own space. Hence there is a sense of awful stillness as well as activity. The noise now begins to fade leaving only the sound of running water.*
*The action now moves between Negrel's office above ground and the trapped miners below ground. Negrel enters closely followed by Dansaert.*

NEGREL:      I was told quite categorically that everything had been checked. Everything.

DANSAERT:    It was Monsieur. I checked most of it myself.

NEGREL:      When?

DANSAERT:    Yesterday.

NEGREL:      Was there any gas when you went down?

DANSAERT:    None.

NEGREL:      And you went everywhere?

DANSAERT:    Aye.

NEGREL:      Well, I don't understand it. Just as things were
             returning to normal. How serious is it?

DANSAERT:    I've seen nowt like this afore. I shouldn't be surprised
             if the pit-head goes.

NEGREL:      Disaster.

DANSAERT:    They're askin' for names Monsieur.

NEGREL:      Have you had a count?

DANSAERT:    Not yet.

NEGREL:      Right. Find someone to do that instantly. Poor devils,
             they'll just have to wait. Have you any idea how many
             there are still down there?

DANSAERT:    Fifty, sixty . . . maybe nowt . . . I don't know.

NEGREL:      They've only themselves to blame, damn it. If this
             strike hadn't happened, the pit would never have been
             allowed to get into this state. As it is, they're going to
             be eaten alive.

DANSAERT:    We'd do best to dig through to the highest face and
             hope they've all made for it together . . .

NEGREL:      But it would take us two weeks man. Is there no other
             way? *(Dansaert shakes his head.)* Very well. It's
             imperative, Dansaert, that we keep utterly silent about
             all this, at least until we know a little more about
             what's actually happened.

DANSAERT:    Aye Monsieur. *(He makes as if to go.)* . . . this may not
             be the time or place Monsieur . . . but I'd just like to
             say how sorry I am about your engagement. . . . I
             understand / from Monsieur . . .

NEGREL:      Yes . . . thank you . . . well, we've other more urgent
             things to worry about now, haven't we . . . don't just
             stand there man, there are lives to be saved!

*Dansaert exits. Lights up on a tunnel at the lowest possible level. Etienne and Catherine are huddled together. There is the sound of water. A lamp burns. They sit in silence. Catherine shivers. Etienne takes his jacket off and puts it round her. He stops in mid-action.*

CATHERINE:  What is it?

*Pause.*

ETIENNE:  Nothing. I thought I heard something.

*They sit and listen. Nothing can be heard. In the course of the following speech we see a light approaching behind them.*

CATHERINE:  Father used to tell stories about this kind o' thing; somehow they were nice when you were lyin' there warm in bed. They were like fairy-tales. . . ; there were allus some hero who came from nowhere and saved everyone. Sometimes though they'd have to wait for days and days wit' nowt food nor water and when they were finally rescued, they stepped out, blinkin' into the daylight, and everyone loved them more than ever, even those as didn't love them afore, and their hair had turned all white. I didn't think it'd happen for real. Not to me. I don't dare / go to sleep . . .

ETIENNE:  Sht! There it is again . . .

*Silence and then a laugh instantly recognisable as Chaval's.*

CHAVAL:  Catherine Levaque! I kent ye were wearyin' for me so I came to find ye . . . (He sees Etienne.) . . . ach, so it was troo. They said ye were doon here. Tae hell wi' that I said. Etienne Lantier? He's a man o' principle, a man wha sticks tae his word . . . ach weel, ye ken what they say don't ye . . . him that's climbed to the top o' the sty drops furthest when he falls . . .

CATHERINE:  Oh God . . .

CHAVAL:  There's no' much he can dae either. I'm all ye ha'e . . . you yin and only hope . . .

ETIENNE:  Is the main shaft still blocked?

CHAVAL:        Do ye think I'd be sat here i'the belly o' the earth with
               ye if it weren't. . . ; there's no way oot. Not unless
               you're a gey guid swimmer. Weel, isn't this just grand!
               The three of us and a' the time i' the world and a wee
               bit mair I expect . . .

               *Silence.*

CATHERINE:     What do we  do now?

ETIENNE:       Sit and wait. If they've any sense at all, they'll work
               out where we are / and start digging straightaway.

CHAVAL:        If they've any noos at all, they'll leave us where we are.
               Hell and Damnation, ye dinnae really think they'll
               spend ower much time and money searchin' for the
               likes of ye . . .

CATHERINE:     You two . . . will you never stop . . .

CHAVAL:        Which'd you rather, that or the silence . . .

CATHERINE:     Neither!

               *Etienne puts his arm around her. Chaval ignores them.
               He sits at some distance from them and takes out a
               piece of bread and lays it ostentatiously in front of
               him. He makes a great show of preparing to eat. The
               others watch.*

CHAVAL:        Ach Catherine, I ken they've been some hard words
               'tween ye and me, and there've been yin or twa
               moments when I've been mebbe a gey bit harsh
               towards ye. But I'm happy tae forgi'e and forget if ye
               are . . . so if you'd like to mebbe share some o' this wi'
               me, you've only tae speak the word . . .

CATHERINE:     What about / him?

ETIENNE:       I'm not hungry.

CHAVAL:        He's no' hungry. *(She shakes her head.)* . . . weel, it's
               up tae ye. I'm no' gaun tae force ye . . .

               *Pause. He continues eating. Catherine watches.*

ETIENNE:       *(Quiet)* Go on. Eat.

CATHERINE:     Nay.

CHAVAL:        It's your last chance. *(He holds up the last piece of his*

*bread. She doesn't respond.)* . . . I tell ye what, we'll
hold on tae this wee yin for later. I reckon ye might
feel hungrier by then . . .

ETIENNE: We'd better move. The water's getting higher.

CHAVAL: In guid time.

ETIENNE: Now.

CHAVAL: If you think you ken the way, go. . . . I'm no' stoppin'
ye, I'd be richt glad tae be rid o' ye. *(They don't move.
Chaval deliberately takes his time getting ready.)* . . .
richt, this way . . .

*He leads them off. Lights up on Negrel's office.*

NEGREL: Etienne Lantier! There must be some mistake.

DANSAERT: One o' the men said he saw him.

NEGREL: That's ridiculous. He must have been mistaken.

DANSAERT: He swears he saw him, wit' the Levaque lass.

NEGREL: How many altogether?

DANSAERT: About forty.

NEGREL: Forty! *(Pause)* Do you have the structural report?

DANSAERT: It's here.

NEGREL: Well?

DANSAERT: We went down last night and spent all o' ten hours in't
main shaft . . .

NEGREL: Yes.

DANSAERT: The linin' had gone. Disappeared in places. As if the
insides had been ripped out; it were nobbut a tangled
mess. We were on our way up again, but I kept feelin'
that summat were wrong somehow, out o' place. So the
others went on up and I stayed a moment and took
another look. *(Pause)*

NEGREL: And?

DANSAERT: The linin' hadn't broken away all jagged as you might
expect, it were all neat and tidy . . .

NEGREL: Yes . . .

DANSAERT:   . . . so that the slightest pressure / and the whole
            place'd . . .

NEGREL:     Are you telling me it had been deliberately cut?

DANSAERT:   Aye Monsieur.

NEGREL:     Do you realise what you're saying man?

DANSAERT:   Indeed I do but I saw it wit' these eyes . . . it'd been
            sawn / in half . . .

NEGREL:     Did anyone else see this?

DANSAERT:   I were the only one.

NEGREL:     Have you mentioned it to anyone?

DANSAERT:   You're the first.

NEGREL:     And the last. Is that clear? I don't want a word of this
            to get out until we know the exact situation.

DANSAERT:   But who could have done such a thing . . . there were
            three hundred and forty hands down there!

NEGREL:     I dread to think. *(Pause)*

DANSAERT:   The first tunnel passed fifteen metres today.

NEGREL:     Fifteen metres. Five metres a day. . . . If they'd dug at
            that rate in the past, none of this would have happened
            in the first instance. *(He laughs.)* A month ago we
            would have had Etienne Lantier hung, drawn and
            quartered. Now it seems we're spending every waking
            minute trying to save his life . . .

            *Lights up on a different tunnel underground, slightly
            higher than the previous one. It is four days later,
            Etienne sits on his own. Catherine kneels next to
            Chaval. Every now and then he feeds her a minute
            mouthful of bread which she has to pay for with a kiss.
            Etienne has a small rock in his hand. He begins to tap
            against the wall.*

CHAVAL:     Ach dinna start wi' that again, will ye . . . *(Etienne
            ignores him.)* We're ower a hundred metres doon; they
            wouldnae hear ye jowlin' at that distance . . . and if
            they daed, when they found us we'd a' be ravin' mad
            frae listenin' tae that for ever and ay. / Leave us alone,
            will ye . . .

CATHERINE:  Let him be . . .

CHAVAL:     That's how it is noo, is it . . . wi' nae food left . . .
            *(Beat)* Well . . . only a half crust. And it'll cost ye mair
            than yin wee kiss. . . ; *(Pause)* It's queer though. The
            hunger has passed away frae me. There's no cravin' noo
            for food. Only water. *(He laughs.)* Only water, I'll lay ye
            ten francs we drown before we starve. *(Etienne stops
            tapping.)* . . . aboot bloody time . . . *(Silence. Etienne
            starts tapping again.)* Christ Almichty! Go and find
            somewhere . . . *(Catherine tries to move away from him.
            He grabs her and pulls her back.)* . . . and where d'ye
            think you're gaun tae? Wha's been feedin' ye for the
            past three days, me or him? *(To Etienne.)* Stop that will
            ye . . . *(To her.)* I'm the gaffer noo, you ken . . .
            Monsieur Hennebeau's right hand man, that's what I
            am. A man o' responsibility, a man o' worth . . . a hard
            man, wha's no' afraid tae tell folk what tae dae, wha
            gets the work done come rain, come shine . . . *(He
            shouts.)* Run for the ladders! *(He laughs.)* Run / for the
            ladders . . .

CATHERINE:  *(To Etienne.)* What's he talkin' about?

CHAVAL:     Ten men i' my team and not yin wha'll lift a finger
            withoot my givin' them the word . . . not yin . . .

CATHERINE:  Etienne . . .

CHAVAL:     What aboot the crust noo . . . mm? Did ye want tae
            pay for it in advance? Just think! That way you can
            ootlive the baith of us . . .

            *He puts his arm around her.*

CATHERINE:  Nay don't.

CHAVAL:     Ay.

CATHERINE:  Nay.

CHAVAL:     Ay, in front o' him. So as I can see his face.

CATHERINE:  Get off!

CHAVAL:     Just like auld times eh . . .

            *Etienne stops tapping.*

ETIENNE:    Leave her alone.

CHAVAL:      If you dinnae like it, turn the other way . . .

             *He kisses Catherine hard on the mouth. She struggles.*

ETIENNE:     Leave her alone or I'll kill you.

CHAVAL:      You've already had that chance. Ye weren't man
             enough tae ta'e it then, so why should ye be noo . . .

             *He pushes Catherine beneath him and tries to take her
             clothes off. Etienne crawls over and very calmly at
             first but building up to a frenzy, smashes Chaval's
             head open with the rock over and over again.
             Catherine screams as Chaval slumps on top of her.*

CATHERINE:   Stop! Stop!

             *He stops out of breath. She wriggles out from beneath
             the body unable to speak. Silence. Etienne rifles
             through Chaval's clothes.*

ETIENNE:     He didn't even have another crust. *(He laughs grimly.)*

             *Lights up on Negrel's office.*

DANSAERT:    Any minute now, Monsieur. We thought you'd better
             be there.

NEGREL:      Of course. Don't expect too much, will you. You've
             seen the conditions down there; it's like a mangled
             carcass.

DANSAERT:    Folk've been known to live for longer than nine
             days . . .

NEGREL:      Without food and drinking-water? *(Pause)* Are the
             families here?

DANSAERT:    Aye, All save Madame Levaque.

NEGREL:      Where's she?

DANSAERT:    She's not moved in nine days. She just sits at home.
             'I'll not shed owt tear over a common blackleg' she
             says; and by all accounts she's not.

NEGREL:      Alright, don't you worry about her, but make sure the
             others are attended to, there's a good fellow. I've heard
             from Paris since we last spoke. They're particularly
             anxious that the exact cause of the . . . incident should
             not become known. Obviously if one person is prepared

to go to such enormous and savage lengths to disrupt
our Industry, there might be others to follow; such
activities must be nipped in the bud. After all, we don't
wish to go around placing ideas in their heads. As far
as you are aware then, apart from the extended
inactivity of the pit as a result of the strike, no clear
reason for the accident is forthcoming. I hope you
appreciate and respect the position of trust in which
you have been placed.

DANSAERT: Aye, Monsieur.

NEGREL: Very well. Let's go.

> *Lights up on the tunnel underground. Again it is
> slightly higher than the previous one. Etienne and
> Catherine are sitting huddled together. The lamp is
> between them, almost extinguished. They both move in
> and out of delirium.*

CATHERINE: Kissin's and beatin's, beatin's and kissin's . . . after a
while I didn't know what I hated most. I'm right glad
he's dead. Is that a wicked thing to say? *(Pause)* I once
thought that if I were to have a day o' doin' nowt, to
rest me a day in some quiet place, it'd maybe set me
up. I were that tired out I thought I'd not enjoy
Heaven without a piece o' rest. But now I've had so
many days of idleness, I'm just as weary o' them as I
were o' my work. Father were right all along, weren't
he . . .

ETIENNE: How?

CATHERINE: To think that there's a Heaven after all. For thee and
me. There is, in't there . . .

ETIENNE: Yes, yes there's a Heaven.

CATHERINE: And a God.

ETIENNE: Yes.

CATHERINE: A God to wipe away all tears. I nobbut think about it
for a half-minute and there I am warmed up all over.

> *She drinks from the water. She screams.*

ETIENNE: What is it?

CATHERINE:   It's him!

ETIENNE:     Who?

CATHERINE:   Chaval! He's followin' us. Won't he ever leave us alone.

ETIENNE:     It can't be.

CATHERINE:   It is. I touched his face, his moustache.

ETIENNE:     *(Reaching out.)* It's the water, he's moved up with the water. I'll push him away.

CATHERINE:   To what use is that?

ETIENNE:     Look, I'm pushing / him away.

CATHERINE:   He'll be back, he'll allus be back, watchin' us, stealin' his kisses.

ETIENNE:     No he won't. There, / he's gone.

CATHERINE:   He'll be back, I say.

ETIENNE:     Not this time, he's gone for ever.

CATHERINE:   No . . .

ETIENNE:     Here, tell me about your Heaven, how is it . . . can / you see . . .

CATHERINE:   Maybe . . .

ETIENNE:     What?

CATHERINE:   Maybe, it weren't him . . . but someone else . . .

ETIENNE:     Who?

CATHERINE:   I don't know . . . *(She exclaims.)*

ETIENNE:     What is it?

CATHERINE:   Of course . . . that's who it is.

ETIENNE:     Who?

CATHERINE:   . . . the Black Miner, come to punish us for ever . . .

ETIENNE:     No . . .

CATHERINE:   Ay, it's him floatin' there, that's who it is. Chaval! all this time, he's the man, o' course . . . *(Pause)* Though he were kind to me once, I remember . . . bought me a ribbon. A blue ribbon. And said I were the prettiest

lass in Montsou. Happen I were then. *(Pause)* I've no
hunger now, nobbut thirst.

ETIENNE: Only a little while longer now. And we'll be there.

CATHERINE: It's lovely outside. Can you see?

ETIENNE: Where?

CATHERINE: Outside. I can. Over there. Over there in the field.
Look! All that green and yellow by the canal and in
front of Monsieur Hennebeau's house; it must be the
early corn growing; of course it's the corn, it's spring
. . . did you ever see so much green, reaching upwards
. . . stretching up to the sky . . . *(Etienne holds her.)* . . .
aye, hold me i' th cornfield. How silly of us to wait all
this time when we would've loved at the very outset.
Do you recall . . . tha thought I were a boy! and then
when tha moved in we couldn't sleep the night for
listenin' to each other's breathin', each darin' the other
to rise and make the first move.

ETIENNE: All we needed was a chance. With no one and nothing
to disturb us. A real chance.

CATHERINE: This is real though, in't it? Here in the sunshine, in the
field with the corn . . .

ETIENNE: Yes, it is.

CATHERINE: Good. Then I'm happy. I've never been so happy. And
alive. Hold me.

ETIENNE: I'm holding you.

CATHERINE: Closer. *(They kiss.)* . . . nay closer. . . .

> *Etienne and Catherine make love in the dim lamplight.*
> *The sounds of spring can be heard in the background*
> *and in the distance the ever-multiplying sound of picks*
> *on coal. These noises crescendo and then fade. Etienne*
> *and Catherine become still. The lights fade on them*
> *leaving only the candle burning on.*

### THE END

## THUNDER IN THE AIR
*August Strindberg*
*Translated by Eivor Martinus*

*'a sulphurous, atmospheric work full of summer lightning'*
GUARDIAN

*£4.95*

## TURCARET
*Alain-René Lesage*
*Translated/adapted by John Norman*

*'One of the best of French comedies'*
SUNDAY TELEGRAPH

*£4.95*

## THERESE RAQUIN
*Emile Zola*
*Translated by Pip Broughton*

*'A gripping yarn'*
GUARDIAN

*£4.95*

## FALSE ADMISSIONS, SUCCESSFUL STRATEGIES, LA DISPUTE
*Marivaux*
*Translated by Timberlake Wertenbaker*

*'the most successful English translator of Marivaux in the present age, if not ever'*
OBSERVER

*£5.95*

# FUENTE OVEJUNA, LOST IN A MIRROR
*Lope de Vega*
*Adapted by Adrian Mitchell*

*'It is hard to imagine a more gripping tale than the one which emerges in Adrian Mitchell's translation'*

TIME OUT

*£5.95*


# THE LIAR, THE ILLUSION
*Pierre Corneille*
*Translated/adapted by Ranjit Bolt*

*Two contrasting plays from one of France's major classic playwrights in an elegant new translation*

*£5.95*


# MAN, BEAST AND VIRTUE
*Luigi Pirandello*
*A new version by Charles Wood*

*'There's no doubting the brilliance of this 1919 farce'*
INDEPENDENT

*£4.95*

# FORTHCOMING TITLES

## THE LULU PLAYS
## THE MARQUIS OF KEITH
*Frank Wedekind*
*Translated and adapted by Steve Gooch*

*Published August 1990*

*£5.95*

## THE WILD DUCK
## JOHN GABRIEL BORKMAN
*Henrik Ibsen*
*Translated by Peter Hall and Inga-Stina Eubank*

*'excellent new translation'*
DAILY TELEGRAPH

*Published September 1990*

*£5.95*

## LUCIFER
*Joost van den Vondel*
*Translated/adapted by Noel Clark*

*'Noel Clark . . . almost persuades you Vondel could out–Milton Milton'*
GUARDIAN

*Published September 1990*

*£4.95*

## THE REAL DON JUAN
*José Zorrilla*
*Translated by Ranjit Bolt*

*Published September 1990*

*£4.95*

# DON JUAN COMES BACK FROM THE WAR
*Translated by Christopher Hampton*
## FIGARO GETS DIVORCED
*Translated by Ian Huish*
*Ödön von Horváth*

*'theatrical poetry as fine as anything since Chekov'*
OBSERVER

*Published October 1990*

*£5.95*